how to grow
ROSES

By JOHN PAUL EDWARDS
Consulting Rosarian, American Rose Society

AND

THE EDITORIAL STAFFS
OF SUNSET MAGAZINE AND BOOKS

Lane Book Company
Menlo Park, California

Beautifully formed flowers of TIFFANY *hold their petals well, are excellent for cutting*

About This Book

This book was written to bring you up to date on roses. Many gardeners are not aware of the changes that have occurred in recent years that make the rose easier to grow and simpler to fit into a modern garden plan than it once was.

Artful hybridizing has produced varieties that are less susceptible to the traditional enemies of the rose, such as mildew, rust, and black spot. New chemicals have made the control of fungi and pests easier and more certain. And the many new types of roses that have been developed, principally in the floribunda class, permit the gardener to absorb the plant into the modern garden. Many landscape architects are freely using massed plantings of flori-bundas in their garden plans. And even the hobbyist can now design a rose garden that doesn't have to mimic the rigid formality of the gardens of Empress Josephine.

In this book, we introduce you to the kinds of roses available and tell you how to buy good plants. You will find ideas for using roses in your garden—whether you have a few plants or an extensive collection. And you will find up-to-date, detailed information on rose culture.

We are grateful to the people who have helped us in the preparation of this manuscript. We would like, in particular, to thank Mr. Clyde Stocking and Dr. Walter Lammerts for their helpful assistance.

Library of Congress Catalog Card Number 55-11802

Title No. 365

SECOND EDITION

Ninth Printing May 1968

Copyright © 1960, 1955

LANE MAGAZINE & BOOK COMPANY, MENLO PARK, CALIFORNIA

Lithographed in the U.S.A.

Top left, Sutter's Gold; *right,* Capistrano; *lower left,* Mission Bells; *right,* Fashion

Contents

CHARLOTTE ARMSTRONG

CHAPTER ONE

The Queen of the Flowers

Since the beginning of history, the rose has held first place in the hearts of man. Ever since humans first became aware of the beauty of flowering plants, the rose has stood head and shoulders above all others. It is grown in every corner of the world where temperate climates exist, and in all probability it will continue to hold first place until the last gardener lays down the last hoe.

You don't have to look far for the reasons—magnificent bursts of bloom in spring and fall with scattered flowering between, richness in color, flower form and fragrance, and a wonderful willingness in the plant to perform under extremes of climate and garden management as long as its few basic needs are satisfied. In the beauty of the individual bloom, the modern hybrid tea is simply unsurpassed. Whether you have one plant or a thousand, there is a special thrill, a special kind of excitement, in every perfect flower.

When you invite the rose to grace your garden, you welcome not only a plant that attains superb beauty but one that proudly carries a rich heritage of legend and history.

The rose is a venerable plant. It is known to have lived and shed its beauty on this earth for many million years before man himself appeared. Fossilized blossoms discovered in Oregon and Colorado have been identified as 35 million—possibly 70 million—years old!

For the colorfully woven history of the rose through the ages of man, we are indebted to a multitude of artists, craftsmen, writers, and plantsmen who have been charmed by this gracious flower and have left a record of their enchantment for future ages to enjoy.

The rose appeared on coins in central Asia as far back as 4,000 B. C., and in Europe it was pictured on frescoes and on coins as early as the 16th century B. C. Architectural rose motifs in Babylonia and Assyria indicate that these civilizations knew the rose. Ancient Coptic manuscripts tell of roses growing in the Hanging Gardens of Babylon.

Greeks Called it "Queen of the Flowers"

Greek poets, historians, and botanists recorded their appreciation of the rose. The poetess Sappho bestowed the title "Queen of the Flowers" upon it in 600 B. C. Homer wrote of the "rosy fingered dawn" in the *Odyssey* and referred to oil of roses in the *Iliad*. The first account of the double rose was reported by Herodotus in the 5th century B. C. The first botanical account of the moss rose was contained in *Enquiry into Plants* written by Theophrastus in the 4th century B. C.

The Greeks brought the rose to the Romans, who took to it enthusiastically, cultivating and importing fine blooms. Pliny, in his natural history, records valuable information concerning the identification of the forms, colors, and growing habits of several roses then in cultivation. During the days of Nero, the decorative uses of roses in Roman festivities reached a point of frenzy. Nero is reported to have spent 4 million sesterces in obtaining roses for a single feast.

There was hardly a public or private Roman ceremony or celebration where the rose was not in evidence. Blossoms were used at weddings, funerals, in conferring military honors, making perfumes, and for medicinal purposes. In powdered or liquid form, the rose was expected to cure a number of unusual ailments, such as bite of the sea dragon, loose teeth, poison of the sea hare, hangovers, watering eyes, and to "wash molligrubs out of a moody brain." Incidentally, medicinal properties of the rose are still being explored. British scientists found during World War II that the rose hip was rich in vitamin C.

Dried roses found in Egyptian tombs of about 300 B. C. are believed to be the first evidence of the Egyptian's acquaintance with the flower. However, researchers are of the opinion that these species were not native to Egypt but were brought there from Asia Minor.

The Rose in Legend and Religious Ceremony

Legends concerning the rose are numerous and varied, depending on the lands, eras, customs, cultures, and faiths from which the traditions arose. Early Mohammedans believed the rose to have been born of a drop of perspiration from the forehead of the Prophet. Legend has it that the Garden of Eden contained white roses, which, when kissed by Eve, turned red and have so remained. The painting "The Birth of Venus" by Botticelli sustains the legend that the rose first appeared when Venus arose from the sea near the island of Cyprus.

Although the Christian Church frowned upon the ways in which the Romans used the rose, it soon took over the flower as a symbol for the survivors of persecution. Since then it has been used in religious ceremonies and paintings, and on ecclesiastical emblems and statuary. Throughout the Middle Ages, rose gardens were carefully tended at English monasteries to provide flowers for ceremonies and processions. Light passing through many stained glass cathedral windows filters through luminous roses embodied in the designs. A famous rose window in the cathedral of York Minster honors the uniting of the houses of York and Lancaster after the War of the Roses.

The Golden Rose of the Church of Rome, dating from the 14th century, is blessed by the Pope on Rose Sunday, and is occasionally bestowed on persons who have distinguished themselves in the Catholic faith.

From the earliest days of chivalry, the rose has been a favored motif for heraldic mottoes, crests, and designs for the banners and shields of knights and sovereigns in England. Several English monarchs adopted the rose as their badge, and it is even now the emblem of England.

Beginnings of the Modern Rose

The start of the 19th century marked the birth of an interest in the rose as a garden flower. This lead to planned creation of new varieties by cross pollinization of existing species and hybrids. New rose authorities, new hybridizers came to the front. Rose gardening as a hobby and a devotion had its inception.

Keenest activity took place in France, thanks partly to the encouragement of Empress Josephine, who became the original great amateur rosarian and patron of the rose. Shortly after 1800, the Empress summoned the leading rose authorities to her gardens at Malmaison. With their aid, she collected all the then-known and available rose varieties, a total of 256.

The Empress also summoned a group of artists to record the form and color of her rose collection. Among these was the "Raphael of the flowers," P. J. Redouté, whose water-color paintings were later published (1817-1824) in a three-volume work, *Les Roses*. Collectors still consider his paintings, or reproductions of them, prized treasures.

The sharpened interest in rose growing stimulated activity in hybridizing, which started a flow of new varieties which has continued to the present day. By 1829, 2,000 named varieties were listed in a contemporary catalog. It is estimated that more than 16,000 named varieties have come and gone in the period from 1815 to date.

The modern rose of today dates its beginnings from the introduction of the *Rosa chinensis* from China to the French Isle of Bourbon. Here, this native of China crossed with *Rosa gallica* to produce the Bourbon rose about 1817. Best known of this strain are SOUVENIR DE MALMAISON and COUPE D' HEBE.

The Bourbons were crossed with *R. damascena* and *R. gallica* and others to produce the great family of roses known as the hybrid perpetuals or June-flowering roses.

Hybrid perpetuals were in turn crossed with an import from China, the tea rose *(R. odorata)* to produce the modern hybrid tea. The first recorded hybrid tea was LA FRANCE, created in France in 1876. The first hybrid teas offered no pure yellow, and it was not until 1900 that this color was achieved by the French hybridizer Joseph Pernet-Doucher, who produced the first of a series of true yellows from which most subsequent yellows have been derived. Roses in this color range are often referred to as Pernetians in reference to their originator.

Today's roses—as discussed in a following chapter—differ greatly from those of the last century. They vary from their ancestors in color, form, fragrance, and length of flowering period. In the early 1800's, all roses bloomed only in the summer, except the Chinese Monthly Rose which also flowered in autumn.

While we have touched the more dramatic phases of the rose's history, let us not forget that the "Queen of the Flowers" has grown in millions of humble gardens. The flower that has been the favorite bloom in the estates of kings can bring beauty and fragrance to your patio, your fence, and the path to your front door.

CHAPTER TWO

Which Is the Rose for You?

When you look over the stock in the nursery bins or browse through the floriferous rose catalogs, you will encounter a generous array of rose plants from which to select. The first time you shop for roses, you might well be puzzled by this display of so many different types and varieties. Fortunately, the range of selection is not so complicated as it may first appear. Once you are acquainted with the characteristics of the main classes and types of roses, you should be able to make your own selections with pleasurable precision.

Nurseries and mail-order dealers group their available stock under two big categories: (1) by plant form—whether bush, tree, or climber; and (2) by class—whether hybrid tea, floribunda, grandiflora, or some older class. Roses in each class are obtainable in one or more of the three plant forms.

In this chapter is a discussion of the rose types, classes, and varieties that are best known on the market, followed by a brief run-down on the rarer varieties which still interest many gardeners even though most of them are hard to find.

TYPES OF GROWTH

In natural habit of growth, the rose is basically a bush. Its canes break low on the plant, grow out and up for 3 feet or more, and terminate in a flower bud. Flowers are borne one to a stem or in clusters of 3 to 5.

Bush roses grow to a height of 2½ to 6 feet or more, depending on variety, culture, pruning methods, and climate. Miniature varieties stop off at 6 to 12 inches. Roses that soar above 6 feet are usually classed as pillars or climbers.

Bush types make up the bulk of the roses sold for garden use by both the amateur and the advanced rosarian. They are planted in groups for borders, beds, foundation screening, or for cut flowers.

Tree Roses

Tree or "standard" roses do not represent a distinct growth habit, but a method of propagation. They are produced by budding bush varieties on specially selected, tall-caned understocks. Any rose, if it is not too vigorous, can be produced as a standard.

Standards are usually 40 to 42 inches tall, but a shorter, 24-inch type is also available for planting in areas with restricted space. They are used to line walks and driveways, to give a formal touch to a rose bed, or to give height and pattern to a garden inclined to flatness.

Because of their long, exposed central cane, standards are fatally sensitive to winter cold. They can be grown in severe-winter areas, but they require special protection to bring them through the frost period.

Climbing Roses

The rose is not a natural climber in the sense that ivy, clematis, or jasmine are climbers. Rose canes have no means for holding on to a vertical surface, such as the holdfasts, tendrils, and other clinging devices that enable vines to climb upward. In a rose, the canes simply continue to grow to 15 or 20 feet or more per season. Trained along a fence, over a trellis, or up a wall, these advancing canes cover vertical surfaces as thoroughly as any true climber. The long, pliant canes have a vegetative bud instead of a flower bud at the tip. Flowers are borne on laterals.

With some species and varieties, this habit of growth is a natural characteristic. Roses like PAUL'S SCARLET, CRIMSOM RAMBLER, BELLE OF PORTUGAL, BLAZE, for instance, are not known to grow in bush form. With others—such as the hybrid teas, floribundas, and grandifloras—the habit is a mutation. Sooner or later the climbing habit occurs in individual specimens of bush roses, and from these plants are taken the stock that produces the marketable climber.

This line-up of roses in containers gives idea of growth habit of the principal classes. Left to right: climbing *hybrid tea, standard hybrid tea, standard floribunda, bush polyantha, floribunda, hybrid tea, and grandiflora*

"Natural" climbers tend to bloom freely, but climbing sports of bush varieties do not bloom so consistently as their bush counterparts. Most climbers are just as sensitive to winter cold as bush roses and require winter protection in areas with severe frost. A few of the "natural" climbers, however, are noted for their hardiness. As a group, climbers require more pruning and winter care than the bush forms. The task of restraining a lusty rambler, for instance, is a real challenge.

Pillar Roses

The pillar falls somewhere between the climber and the bush rose. Perhaps it is best described as a very long caned bush type that grows to 8 feet or more. Canes are not pliable like those of the climbers but grow erect without support. Unlike the climbing habit that is a sport of the bush form, the pillar habit is a definite characteristic of the pillar varieties. In some localities, the pillar is known as a "semi-climber," a name that recognizes the reluctance of these roses to grow as vigorously as the other climbers.

Pillars are usually trained against a post or pillar and are used along porches, on lamp posts, or mixed in with other plants for a spectacular display of concentrated color.

Pillars as a group are fairly hardy, but they require heavy pruning of laterals to keep in pillar form.

CLASSES OF ROSES

Today's roses are, of course, descended from ancient species roses—single-flowered, spring-blooming, brambly plants growing wild in temperate areas of the world. Because garden roses are as old as gardening, they have been tinkered with, hybridized, selected, crossed and back-crossed for generations. The family tree of today's roses, fundamental to any botanical system of classification, is extremely complicated—in fact, it is well beyond the scope of this book.

Here are the classes of roses most widely planted today—the kinds you are likely to find in the catalogs and nurseries as bare-root stock in mid-winter or as container plants during the growing season. Other classes—those not so easily obtained and not so widely grown—are discussed in a following section.

Within each of the classes briefly discussed below, are innumerable hybrids and varieties. Of these, a hundred sure-fire varieties are evaluated in the chart.

Hybrid Tea

The hybrid tea is probably the best loved and most frequently grown of all roses, outselling all other classes combined.

The hybrid tea is a cross between two older roses—the hybrid perpetual, which dominated the rose world from 1840 to 1890, and the tea rose, a vigorous, everblooming hybrid that was imported from China in the 18th Century.

1955 All-America Selections are exception to general rule that hybrid teas are larger than floribundas, *grandifloras. Left to right: grandiflora* QUEEN ELIZABETH; *hybrid tea* TIFFANY; *floribunda* JIMINY CRICKET

Both hybrid perpetuals and tea roses can still be obtained in a limited selection from specialty nurseries. They are discussed in more detail in the section on Old-Fashioned Roses.

Intensive research in the past 20 years has resulted in enormous progress in improving hybrid teas: the newer varieties are big-growing, vigorous, and fairly disease resistant. Ideally, they produce large, beautifully formed flowers and long, graceful buds. CHARLOTTE ARMSTRONG, perhaps the most important hybrid tea developed in the West, has given rise to a long line of award-winning descendents.

Hybrid teas are offered in a wide color selection, including many shades of red, yellow, orange, pink, and pure white. These are the roses of the formal garden, the cutting bed, and the florist's greenhouse.

Climbing and pillar types of hybrid teas are available for many—but not all—varieties. Their blooms are similar to those of the bush varieties, but some are slightly smaller and they usually do not bloom so continuously.

Most tree roses are hybrid teas.

Floribundas and Polyanthas

These are the smaller-flowered, low-growing roses that bear flowers in masses almost continuously during spring and summer. They carry traits of hardiness and disease resistance from a set of ancestors entirely separate from those of the hybrid teas. Rose breeders are turning more and more to floribundas for these valuable traits, injecting

them into the hybrid tea line with various crosses. In recent years, floribundas have won several All-America Rose Selections awards.

Polyanthas are, of course, old-timers in the rose garden —nearly everyone is familiar with CECILE BRUNNER (1881) or BABY ROSE. Polyanthas produce small flowers (less than 2″ diameter) in large clusters. Although the color range is limited and the blossoms are not noted for fragrance, the plants are hardy and may be grown in localities that are too cold for hybrid teas. Only a few polyanthas as such are still in commerce—notably, MARGO KOSTER, THE FAIRY, and the durable CECILE BRUNNER —for their place has been pretty well usurped by the floribundas.

The *floribunda* is a relatively new type—introduced in 1924—produced from crossing hybrid teas with polyanthas. These roses carry hybrid tea blood in varying amounts, producing bigger flowers than the polyanthas and bearing them in both sprays and clusters. With many of them, the flowers are perfect miniatures of the flowers of hybrid teas. PINOCCHIO is a good example. Indeed, some varieties are so close to hybrid teas in appearance that the amateur finds them difficult to tell apart. Some of the earlier floribundas were lacking in fragrance, but more recent introductions have improved on this deficiency. Nearly all the colors obtainable in hybrid teas are now available in floribundas.

Despite their newness, floribundas have gained a firm position, for they have many characteristics that commend

9

them to the home gardener: Probably no shrubs in the nursery can equal them in their bright display of continuous color. Unlike the more formal hybrid teas, they are adaptable to a variety of garden uses. They make attractive foundation plants, fit pleasantly into borders, and can even be blended with perennials and shrubs. They can be used as hedges and borders, and base plantings around sundials, garden lamp posts, tree roses, etc. Some varieties can even be induced to grow happily in tubs or large pots. They are most effective if planted in solid masses of the same color and kind, spaced fairly close together.

Like hybrid teas, the floribundas have their share of climbing types. Their flowers are mostly identical with those on the bush forms from which they have developed, and their bloom is fairly continuous. Although hardier than climbing hybrid teas, they too require protection in severe winter areas. With their massed blooms, they provide spectacular color on walls, fences, and trellises.

A few varieties of floribundas are obtainable as standards, such as LILIBET, JIMINY CRICKET, FRENSHAM, and others, but as a rule, this form of growth is left to the hybrid teas.

Grandifloras

This is a class of roses resulting from crosses between the floribundas and hybrid teas. Grandifloras combine many of the best features of both parents. The plants are vigorous, some varieties growing to 6 feet or more, with blooms that approach the hybrid teas in quality. Flowers, which are borne both in clusters and singly on long stems, are slightly smaller than hybrid tea blossoms, but they share the same perfection of bud and flower form. Grandifloras carry the everblooming habits, hardiness, and disease resistance of the old polyantha types.

At present, only a handful of varieties make up this expanding class. As more are developed, the gardener will be able to choose climbers, standards, and pillars in a wide range of colors. Despite their small number, several grandifloras have already won AARS awards.

NATURAL CLIMBERS

In addition to the climbing hybrid teas, floribundas, and grandifloras, there is another large group of climbers that contains several old favorites, such as PAUL'S SCARLET, EVANGELINE, CRIMSON RAMBLER, and others. Many of the varieties within this group are difficult if not impossible to obtain, but a few of them are still listed in every rose catalog. These climbers group themselves, roughly, into three classes:

Ramblers

Ramblers are prodigious growers. Each year they produce many long, vigorous basal canes that may reach 15 or 20 feet in a season. They are useful for covering large wall areas, fences, and walls. Their vigor rules them out of most small gardens, unless the gardener is able to keep them in bounds with relentless pruning.

Ramblers bear their small (under 2 inches) flowers in dense clusters, usually in June on wood produced the previous season. Their color range covers all the standard colors but yellow. Although they are not affected by winter cold, many varieties are quite susceptible to mildew. For this reason, they are being displaced in the nurseries by newer climbing types that are less subject to mildew and that produce larger blooms.

Typical varieties: DOROTHY PERKINS (white), CRIMSON RAMBLER.

Large-flowered Climbers

Unlike the ramblers, roses in this group are adapted to use in small gardens. Because they grow slowly, they produce sturdy canes and bloom on 2-year wood. They do require heavy annual pruning and can be kept in bounds. They are easily trained to grow up a post or a trellis or along a fence. The flowers of some varieties are large and handsome—well suited to cutting.

Typical old favorites: PAUL'S SCARLET CLIMBER, CITY OF YORK, BELLE OF PORTUGAL, DR. W. VAN FLEET.

Everblooming Climbers

Roses in this group are actually far from "everblooming," although they do break forth with a profusion of blossoms in late spring and early summer and then bloom intermittently through the balance of summer and fall. In some climates, a second season of generous bloom occurs in autumn. Many of the varieties in this class, such as NEW DAWN, DR. J. H. NICOLAS, so closely resemble hybrid tea climbers in appearance and growth habits, that they are often classed as such. Climbers in this group, however, are hardy in cold climates.

Typical varieties: In addition to the two mentioned above, BLAZE (red), PENELOPE (white).

TRAILERS

Trailing roses are climbers with very pliable canes that creep along the ground. They are even adapted to planting on walls and banks and are sometimes used as a ground cover. Their flowers are not notably attractive. They are hardy in cold climates. (Cont. on page 25.)

Hybrid Tea: LA JOLLA

Grandiflora: ROUNDELAY

Floribunda: LILIBET

Polyantha: PINKIE

CHART OF RECOMMENDED VARIETIES

This chart is intended primarily to provide a list of representative roses that can be grown successfully in almost every rose-growing area of the country.

In preparing this list, we consulted prominent rose growers in sixteen widespread, key regions of the country. These experts selected from a long list of the best modern roses the ones that are grown successfully in their areas. We then checked their reports against the findings of the American Rose Society.

AARS

A rose that has been chosen as an All-America Rose Selection is indicated by AARS in parentheses below the name. All-America Roses are selected each year from new roses grown in 22 trial gardens throughout the country over a period of two years.

HYBRID TEAS—RED

Name	Color	Fragrance	Disease Resistance	Height	Habit of Growth	Climate Adaptability	Comments
CHAS. MALLERIN	Very dark red	Fine old fragrance	Resistant, some mildew	3-4'	Upright	General	Magnificent deep red rose. Full blown flower is lovely, never fades blue. A strong grower and a fair producer of blooms.
CHARLOTTE ARMSTRONG (AARS)	Red to dark pink	Light fragrance	Resistant	3-4'	Upright, spreading	General, best color in warm climates	One of finest roses ever produced. A strong grower, producing abundance of excellent blooms. Long, pointed buds open to large, well formed flowers.
CHRYSLER IMPERIAL (AARS)	True red	Fragrant	Resistant, some mildew	3-4'	Upright, compact	General, blues in cold, wet weather	A magnificent red. High-centered bud opens to a 40 to 50-petal bloom of fine substance. Dark green foliage covers plant from ground up.
CRIMSON GLORY	Velvety crimson	Very fragrant	Some mildew	3-4'	Spreading	Best in warm climates	Rated as finest of all reds in some sections of the country. Beautiful flowers of perfect form. Vigorous, bushy plant. Continuous bloomer.
ENA HARKNESS	Rich red	Fragrant	Some mildew	2½-3'	Upright, spreading	Best in cool areas	An English rose, very popular in that country. Blooms have velvety texture. Good cutting rose.
ETOILE DE HOLLANDE	Dark velvety red	Very fragrant	Some mildew	3-4'	Upright, spreading	General	One of the best of reds; color rarely blues. A favorite everywhere. Excellent cutting rose.
MISTER LINCOLN (AARS)	Rich Red	Very fragrant	Resistant	4-6'	Upright	General	1965 All-America. Long tapering buds open to form rich velvety red blooms up to 6 inches across, excellent for cutting. Vigorous grower.
NEW YORKER	Rich red	Some fragrance	Mildews slightly	3-4'	Upright	General	An attractive double rose that rarely blues. Long sturdy stems. Excellent for cutting. A vigorous plant that blooms profusely.
NOCTURNE (AARS)	Dark red	Fragrant	Mildews except in warm areas	3-3½'	Upright	Not for coastal areas	Buds are long, streamlined, very dark red with blackish sheen. Strong, bushy plant with dark green foliage. Wonderful in warm, dry areas.
ROYAL VELVET	Dark velvety red	Sweet fragrance	Mildews slightly	4'	Upright	General	A lovely dark shade of red. Vigorous. Its long stems sometimes bend from weight of large flowers.
TEXAS CENTENNIAL	Light red	Very fragrant	Mildews slightly	5-6'	Upright	General	A sport of President Hoover. Produces many large blooms of exhibition quality. A vigorous grower and a satisfactory rose in every way.

HYBRID TEAS—ORANGE TONES

Name	Color	Fragrance	Disease Resistance	Height	Habit of Growth	Climate Adaptability	Comments
AZTEC	Scarlet orange	Fragrant	Resistant	2-3'	Spreading	General	A giant flaming orange flower of exhibition form, long lasting color. Vigorous, handsomely foliaged plant. New color; a great favorite.
GAIL BORDEN	Pink, red, apricot	Slight fragrance	Disease resistant	3½-5'	Upright	General	A truly glamorous, large, high centered flower of superb open beauty. Up to 70 petals. Luxuriant dark shiny foliage.
LADY ELGIN	Orange-buff	Fragrant	Disease resistant	4-5'	Upright	General	Large handsome bud and flower of a new, dark gold color. Long stems for cutting. A vigorous, tall plant with attractive foliage.
MOJAVE (AARS)	Tones of orange	Slight fragrance	Resistant	3-4'	Upright	General	Has the rich colorings of a desert sunset. Produces many long-stemmed, richly colored flowers of great beauty. A fine cutting rose.
MRS. SAM McGREDY	Coppery salmon, rose-pink	Fragrant	Mildews slightly	3-4'	Upright, spreading	General	The favorite rose of many rosarians. Large, pointed buds open to a double bloom. The glossy foliage is a dark olive green. Fine for cutting and arrangements.
SIGNORA	Burnt sienna, orange, and cerise	Slight fragrance	Resistant	4-5'	Upright	General	A fine Italian rose. Long buds of warm burnt sienna open to a lighter hue. Plant is a strong, vigorous grower with fine foliage. Flowers are borne on long stems.
TANYA	Orange	Slight fragrance	Resistant	3½-4'	Upright	General	An entirely new shade of rich orange. Flower color varies from apricot orange to burnt orange, depending on region where it is grown. Large flowers, to 5½ inches. Generous bloomer.
TAPESTRY	Orange-yellow-red blend	Spicy fragrance	Disease resistant	2-3'	Spreading	General	Flowers are a rich mixed blend of warm colors. A low growing but handsome bush. Fine glossy foliage. In every way a choice new rose.
TROPICANA (AARS)	Reddish orange	Fragrant	Resistant	3-6'	Spreading	General	1963 All-America. Many experts believe this offspring of Peace is destined to become one of the greatest favorites of them all. Abundant bloomer; exceptional for cutting.

HYBRID TEAS—PINK

Name	Color	Fragrance	Disease Resistance	Height	Habit of Growth	Climate Adaptability	Comments
CAPISTRANO (AARS)	Deep rose-pink	Strong, fruity fragrance	Resistant	5-6'	Upright	General	Bushy, upright plant produces abundance of large buds. Foliage is leathery and clothes the plant well.
COUNTESS VANDAL	Pink to buff	Fragrant	Mildews slightly in cool areas	2½-4'	Upright	General	Bronze-pink buds open to lovely, large, high-centered blooms of blended carmine, pink, buff, gold. A fine cutting rose.
DAINTY BESS	Dusky pink	Slight fragrance	Some mildew	3-4'	Upright	General	Most popular of the singles. A good cut flower if cut in tight bud. An old favorite.
DUET (AARS)	Pink	Slight fragrance	Resistant	3½'	Upright, spreading	General	1961 All-America. Outside of petals a rosy pink, inside petals a softer tone. Easy to grow, blooms freely throughout the season.
FIRST LOVE	Dawn pink	Slight fragrance	Resistant	3½-4½'	Upright, spreading	General	Lovely long, slender buds. Flowers are a rose-pink shading to dawn pink. Blooms profusely. A fine rose for cuttings and arrangements.
HELEN TRAUBEL (AARS)	Apricot pink	Mild fragrance	Resistant	4-5'	Upright, spreading	General	Large, vigorous plant. Produces quantities of luminous apricot to sparkling pink blooms. Long, tapering buds.
MICHELE MEILLAND	Shell pink, salmon	Mild fragrance	Mildews slightly	2½-3'	Upright, spreading	General	Exhibition-type blooms of an exquisite soft shell pink coloring. Blooms heavily on a fine spreading plant. Makes a lovely cutting flower.
MISSION BELLS (AARS)	Salmon pink	Slight fragrance	Resistant	3-4'	Upright, spreading	General	Buds of deep salmon open to big, full blooms of shrimp pink. Tall, vigorous plant nearly always in bloom. Likes sun.
PICTURE	Rose-pink, undertone of salmon	Slight fragrance	Mildews slightly	2½-3½'	Upright	General	One of the best and most reliable pinks. Medium sized, high-centered bloom. Grows well and blooms freely.
PINK DUCHESS	Deep pink	Sweet fragrance	Resistant	3½-4½'	Upright, spreading	General	Blooms are a shimmering, glowing dark pink. Should be disbudded to make room for the huge flowers. Sturdy, bushy plant.
PINK PEACE	Deep pink	Mild fragrance	Mildews slightly	4-5'	Upright	General	Tall, sturdy plant with heavy foliage that produces quantities of large blooms borne singly on long stems. Flowers have wavy petals.
ROYAL HIGHNESS (AARS)	Light pink	Fragrant	Resistant	4-5'	Upright	General	1963 All-America. Medium-sized flowers, borne in abundance. Luxuriant foliage. Pleasing fragrance. A seedling of Peace.
THE DOCTOR	Light pink	Intensely fragrant	Mildews slightly	2½-3'	Upright	General	A moderate-sized bush producing very large, true pink flowers. Not the easiest rose to grow, but well worth the effort.
TIFFANY (AARS)	Silvery pink flushed gold	Very fragrant	Resistant	3-4'	Upright	General, best in warm areas	A beautiful rose with silvery pink blooms flushed yellow at the base. Perfectly formed blooms are borne singly on long stems ideal for cutting.

HYBRID TEAS—YELLOW

Name	Color	Fragrance	Disease Resistance	Height	Habit of Growth	Climate Adaptability	Comments
ECLIPSE	Yellow	Some fragrance	Resistant	3-4'	Upright	General	Elegant, streamlined buds are borne on long, straight stems. Fine for cutting in the tight bud. Vigorous plant.
FRED HOWARD (AARS)	Yellow blend	Slight fragrance	Resistant	5-6'	Upright	General	A well formed bloom borne on a vigorous plant. Bloom opens well, has fine keeping qualities. Balls some in damp weather.
ISOBEL HARKNESS	Yellow	Some fragrance	Resistant	3'	Upright	General	Beautifully formed, long, pointed bud opens to a large, wide petalled, high-centered bloom. An exhibition flower. Glossy foliage.
KING'S RANSOM (AARS)	Yellow	Fragrant	Resistant	5-6'	Upright	General	1962 All-America. May eventually replace Eclipse as the standard-bearer among the yellows. Tall, vigorous plant with large blooms that hold their color in rain or sun.
LOWELL THOMAS (AARS)	Yellow	Good fragrance	Resistant	3-3½'	Upright	General	A truly reliable yellow. Finely formed buds open to rich yellow blooms of good form and substance. Strong grower. Dark green foliage.

HYBRID TEAS—WHITE

Name	Color	Fragrance	Disease Resistance	Height	Habit of Growth	Climate Adaptability	Comments
FRAU KARL DRUSCHKI	Pure white	Slight fragrance	Fair, some mildew	4-5'	Upright, spreading	Best in warm areas	A fine old hybrid perpetual. Long, pointed buds open to large blooms. Repeats well in some climates. Big bush; a real eye-catcher.
MATTERHORN (AARS)	Ivory White	No fragrance	Resistant	5-6'	Upright	General	1966 All-America. Long, well-formed buds, medium-sized flowers. Grows and blooms with a vigor unusual for a white rose.
SNOWBIRD	White	Slight fragrance	Resistant	2-3'	Spreading	General	One of the best white roses. Medium sized buds. Fine, high-centered blooms. Foliage is excellent and plant blooms freely.
VIRGO	White	Slight fragrance	Resistant	3-3½'	Upright	General	Beautiful streamlined buds open to pure white, medium-sized blooms. Vigorous, free-flowering. One of the best whites for cutting.
WHITE KNIGHT (AARS)	Pure white	Mild fragrance	Mildews slightly	3-4'	Upright	General	The first white hybrid tea rose to win an All-America award. Pure white, satiny flowers of excellent form, borne singly on long stems good for cutting. Vigorous plant, free-branching.

WHICH ROSE FOR YOU?

HYBRID TEAS—BICOLORS AND BLENDS

Name	Color	Fragrance	Disease Resistance	Height	Habit of Growth	Climate Adaptability	Comments
AMERICAN HERITAGE (AARS)	Ivory yellow, tinged salmon and scarlet	Slight fragrance	Mildews slightly	5-7′	Upright	General	1966 All-America. Flowers large and full (petal count: 50-60); petals remain upright, covering flower's center. Tones of red in foliage.
CHICAGO PEACE	Pink-coppery blend	Slight fragrance	Resistant	5′	Upright spreading	General	This 1962 introduction is a true sport of Peace, with the same outstanding qualities. The large, impressive blooms are a blend of deep pink, yellow, and copper.
FASCINATING	Crimson and yellow	Some fragrance	Disease resistant	3-4′	Bushy, upright	General	High-centered blooms, with 25 petals, are a delightful blend of crimson and yellow. Truly a fascinating rose, exciting in any garden.
GARDEN PARTY (AARS)	White, pink shadings	Fragrant	Resistant	4-5′	Upright, spreading	General	The 1960 All-America winner. Flowers are a rich ivory at the center, shading out to creamy tones and apple blossom pink. Long, lovely buds open to high centers and exhibition-type blooms. Vigorous, free-branching plant.
GRANADA (AARS)	Scarlet, red, yellow	Sweet fragrance	Mildews slightly	4′	Upright, spreading	General	1964 All-America. Perfectly formed semi-double flowers. Best cut in tight bud. Leaves are dark green, holly-like.
MARK SULLIVAN	Yellow and cerise	Fragrant	Resistant	4-5′	Spreading	Best in warm climates	A stunning rose with a dazzling color scheme of golden yellow, rose pink, and cerise. A strong, bushy, free-flowering plant.
PEACE (AARS)	Yellow shaded cerise	Delicate fragrance	Resistant	3½-5′	Upright, spreading	General	One of the finest roses ever produced. Large buds open to huge flowers, no two of which are exactly alike. Vigorous, with excellent dark green foliage, sturdy stems. Free flowering if pruned lightly.
PRESIDENT HOOVER	Orange-pink-buff	Fragrant	Mildews slightly	5-6′	Upright	General	A strong grower with blooms borne on long, sturdy stems. Long buds open to large blooms. Fine for cutting.
SUSPENSE	Red and yellow	Slight fragrance	Mildew free	4-5′	Upright	General	Magnificent blooms are 6 inches across with 40 to 60 substantial petals. Long, strong stems for cutting. Buds—usually one to a stem—are a soft yellow; open flowers are a deep red.
SUTTER'S GOLD (AARS)	Yellow shaded orange	Very fragrant	Resistant	4-5′	Upright, spreading	General	An exquisite rose in every way. Long, pointed bud opens to fine, large bloom. Tall, vigorous plant is a heavy and continuous bloomer.

HYBRID TEAS—OTHER COLORS

Name	Color	Fragrance	Disease Resistance	Height	Habit of Growth	Climate Adaptability	Comments
FANTAN	Brownish tan	Slight fragrance	Resistant	3′	Upright	Likes cooler climates	Grows well with generous quantity of blooms. The flowers have long stems, and because of their unique color are interesting to flower arrangers.
SIMONE	Clear pastel lilac	Slight fragrance	Resistant	3-4′	Upright, spreading	Likes dry location	Has an immense bloom of 50-60 petals, usually 6 inches in diameter. Holds its color well. One of the best of the new lilac-colored roses.
STERLING SILVER	Silvery lavender	Fragrant	Resistant	3′	Upright	General	Beautifully formed flower of a new color—silvery lavender. Nearly every flower is perfect. Vigorous, heavy blooming plant with handsome foliage. A truly great new rose.

FLORIBUNDAS—RED

Name	Color	Fragrance	Disease Resistance	Height	Habit of Growth	Climate Adaptability	Comments
FIRE KING (AARS)	Brilliant vermilion	Slight fragrance	Mildews slightly	3-4′	Upright, spreading	General	1960 All-America. Long lasting, fiery red double blooms grow singly and in clusters. Fine for cutting. Vigorous grower.
FLORADORA (AARS)	Scarlet-orange	No fragrance	Mildews slightly	4-5′	Upright	General	Profuse blooms are borne on vigorous plant in small clusters. Excellent bronzy foliage.
FRENSHAM	Deep crimson red	Mild fragrance	Resistant	3-4′	Upright, spreading	General	A superb floribunda that produces masses of unfading blooms. Buds open to well formed, open flowers with golden stamens. Glossy foliage covers plant well.
FUSILIER (AARS)	Iridescent vermilion	Fragrant	Resistant	2½-3½′	Upright, full	General	A worthy All-America, highly recommended. Lovely dark red flowers that cut and last well. Vigorous, well foliaged plant.
GARNETTE	Garnet red	No fragrance	Mildews	2-3′	Upright, massing	Likes heat	Great favorite of the florists; flowers last a week to 10 days indoors. Good for border. Masses of holly-like foliage. Must be sprayed frequently to prevent mildew, but well worth it.
RED PINOCCHIO	Red	No fragrance	Mildews slightly	3-3½′	Spreading	General	Deep, satiny, carmine buds open to rich clear red flower of hybrid tea form. Extremely hardy plant, easy to grow and almost always in bloom.
SARABANDE (AARS)	Oriental red	Slight fragrance	Mildews slightly	2½-3′	Low, spreading	General	1960 All-America. Probably the most brilliant red of any rose grown, and the color lasts. Semi-double flowers. Heavy, almost constant bloom.

FLORIBUNDAS—RED (Continued)

Name	Color	Fragrance	Disease Resistance	Height	Habit of Growth	Climate Adaptability	Comments
SIREN	Fiery scarlet	No fragrance	Mildews slightly	2½-3′	Upright, spreading	General	Blazing red blooms last until the charming, ruffled petals drop. Vigorous.
SPARTAN (AARS)	Warm orange-red	Sweet old-rose fragrance	Resistant	2½-3½′	Upright, spreading	General	Very fine floribunda. Yields a profusion of large, perfectly formed blooms of 35-40 petals. Vigorous plant. Blooms continuously.
VOGUE (AARS)	Cherry coral	Spicy fragrance	Resistant	2½-3½′	Upright, spreading	General	A great favorite. Flowers have a high-centered, lovely form. Plants are ideal for hedges, foundation plantings, or massed color in beds.

FLORIBUNDAS—PINK

Name	Color	Fragrance	Disease Resistance	Height	Habit of Growth	Climate Adaptability	Comments
BETTY PRIOR	Carmine to shell pink	No fragrance	Resistant	4-5′	Upright, spreading	General	Persistent bloomer, usually a mass of color. Buds are lively red opening to shell pink. Blooms resemble pink dogwood in shape, size, color. Strong-growing plant. Leathery foliage.
FASHION	Coral-pink	Fragrant	Mildews slightly	2½-3′	Upright, spreading	General	An exquisite floribunda of a unique, luminous coral-pink coloring. Plants are bushy and well foliaged. A lovely cut flower.
FASHIONETTE	Coral-pink	Very fragrant	Resistant	2½-3½′	Upright, spreading	General	At last a truly fragrant floribunda. Fully petalled flower rivals shape of hybrid tea. Blooms both singly and in clusters. Dark green, glossy, bountiful foliage. Best floribunda of its color.
LILIBET (AARS)	Dawn pink	Slight fragrance	Resistant	2-3′	Spreading	General	Compact, bushy plant with deep reddish green, glossy foliage. Excellent rose for corsages and arrangements. Makes an excellent low hedge.
MA PERKINS (AARS)	Soft coral shell pink	Mild fragrance	Resistant	2-3′	Upright, spreading	General	Generously blooming bush; a sturdy, compact grower with rich green foliage. Blooms hold color well, make lovely corsages and bouquets.
PINKIE (AARS)	Pink	No fragrance	Very resistant	1½-2′	Compact	General	A dwarf rose, fine for low hedges and edgings. Lovely, pointed buds open to pale pink, semi-double flowers. Blooms almost continuously and has many decorative uses.
PINOCCHIO	Salmon pink	Fruity fragrance	Resistant	2½-3½′	Spreading	General	Large clusters of pointed buds open to long-lasting, well formed blooms of soft pink shaded deeper at edges. Hardy plant with dark green foliage. Good for mass planting and edgings.
ROSENELFE	Clear pink	Slight fragrance	Resistant	3-4′	Upright	General	One of the best floribundas for cutting and arrangements. Makes a lovely hedge. Long-lasting blooms. Vigorous. Dark green foliage.

FLORIBUNDAS—WHITE

Name	Color	Fragrance	Disease Resistance	Height	Habit of Growth	Climate Adaptability	Comments
IVORY FASHION (AARS)	Ivory white	Sweet fragrance	Resistant	2-3′	Upright, spreading	General	Unique in form, coloring. Long, slender buds open to high-centered, soft-ivory flower; when fully open, bloom reveals a nest of golden stamens. Blooms hold color to the last. Full foliaged.
SARATOGA (AARS)	Ivory white	Mild fragrance	Resistant	2½-3′	Upright, spreading	General	1964 All-America. Buds borne singly or in clusters. Gardenia-like flowers have cluster of golden stamens in center.

FLORIBUNDAS—OTHER COLORS

Name	Color	Fragrance	Disease Resistance	Height	Habit of Growth	Climate Adaptability	Comments
APRICOT NECTAR (AARS)	Apricot	Fruity fragrance	Resistant	2½-3′	Spreading	General	1966 All-America. Apricot buds lighten slightly as they open to a high-centered flower, 4½ to 5 inches across. Repeat bloom is quick and abundant.
CIRCUS (AARS)	Orange-buff-pink	No fragrance	Resistant	2½-3′	Upright, spreading	General	The everchanging colors vary from rich yellow and red in the bud to orange-buff flushed with red or pink in the flower. Large, glossy foliage enhances the beauty of this fine plant.
GOLD CUP (AARS)	Deep yellow	Sweet fragrance	Resistant	3′	Upright, spreading	General	Generally regarded as the best of the yellow floribundas. Well formed bloom lasts well as a cut flower. Good bush, glossy dark foliage.
GOLDEN SLIPPERS (AARS)	Orange and gold	Slight fragrance	Resistant	2′	Spreading	General	1962 All-America. Gay colors; good foreground planting. Blooms drop petals cleanly and all at once as new bud clusters replace them.
JIMINY CRICKET (AARS)	Coral-orange to coral-pink	Mild fragrance	Resistant	2½-3½′	Upright, spreading	General	Flowers are borne singly and in clusters on compact, bushy plant. A fine cutting flower.
LITTLE DARLING	Yellow, pink, orange	Fragrant	Resistant	4-5′	Upright, spreading	General	A "must" for every garden. A heavy, continuous bloomer, tops for cutting. Appealing form and color. Well fed can make a "pillar climber." Blooms singly and in clusters. Order early.

GRANDIFLORAS

Name	Color	Fragrance	Disease Resistance	Height	Habit of Growth	Climate Adaptability	Comments
BUCCANEER	Golden yellow	Slight fragrance	Resistant	5-7'	Upright	General	This fine rose has a clear golden color that does not fade. Plants are extremely vigorous growing to 5 or 6 feet when established. Foliage is a rich green and clothes the entire plant.
CAMELOT (AARS)	Vibrant coral pink	Spicy fragrance	Resistant	5-6'	Upright	General	1965 All-America. The 5-inch flowers open from rounded buds in large clusters. A tall and vigorous grower. Excellent heavy foliage.
CARROUSEL	Vivid dark red	Fragrant	Resistant	3-4'	Upright, spreading	General	Fully opened flowers are 3 to 4 inches in diameter and hold their color well. Good cutting flower. Vigorous plant.
EL CAPITAN	Light red	Some fragrance	Mildews slightly	4-5'	Upright, spreading	General	Nicely formed blooms of a light currant red. A vigorous plant, producing many flowers singly and in clusters. Blooms hold color well.
GOLDEN GIRL	Clear yellow	Slight fragrance	Resistant	3-4'	Spreading	General	Very heavy production of beautifully formed blooms of hybrid tea quality. Blooms hold clear yellow color best if plant is in partial shade. A new rose that may prove to be best of yellows.
MONTEZUMA	Burnt orange tones	Slight fragrance	Resistant	3-4'	Upright	General	Notable for its rich orange-buff colorings. A vigorous plant well clothed with foliage. As a cutting rose, has few if any superiors.
PINK PARFAIT (AARS)	Pink blend	Slight fragrance	Resistant	4'	Upright, spreading	Best in cooler areas	1961 All-America. Blooms, smaller than most grandifloras, are a blend of delicate pinks. Very free flowering.
QUEEN ELIZABETH (AARS)	Delicate clear pink	Mild fragrance	Very resistant	5-6'	Upright	General	Tall, stately plant with blooms of lovely coloring. High-centered blooms of hybrid tea form are borne singly and in clusters on almost thornless stems. Extremely vigorous plants produce a profusion of blooms. Glossy foliage.
ROUNDELAY	Dark red	Fragrant	Resistant	5'	Upright, spreading	Best in dryer climates	Blooms of lasting quality, fine for cutting. Good bud form. Vigorous, free flowering, a continuous bloomer. Excellent rose when it gets its roots.
STARFIRE (AARS)	Currant red	Slight fragrance	Resistant	4-6'	Upright, spreading	General	A rose lover's rose. Lovely currant red color that is sunfast. Blooms singly and in clusters on 6 to 12-inch stems. A truly great rose.

CLIMBERS AND PILLAR TYPES

Name	Color	Fragrance	Disease Resistance	Yearly Height	Climate Adaptability	Comments
BLAZE	Scarlet	Slight fragrance	Slight mildew	10-15'	General	Called "the everblooming Paul's Scarlet." Gives great masses of vivid, double scarlet blooms over a long period.
CLG. CARROUSEL	Dark red	Not fragrant	Mildews slightly	7-10'	General	Flower is a very lovely dark red, identical to that of the grandiflora form. Stems are long enough for cutting. Repeat bloomer.
CLG. CECILE BRUNNER	Light pink	Fragrant	Slight mildew	20-30'	Best in mild climate	The "sweetheart rose." Most popular of the baby roses. Blooms profusely in clusters almost continuously.
CLG. CRIMSON GLORY	Dark red	Very fragrant	Mildews slightly	9-11'	Best in warm areas	Fine red climber for warm areas. Well formed blooms are produced freely over a long period.
CLG. ETOILE DE HOLLANDE	Deep red	Fragrant	Resistant	15-20'	South, far west coastal areas	Most satisfactory of the red climbers. Does quite well in most areas, best in south and western coastal areas.
CLG. MRS. SAM McGREDY	Coppery red to salmon	Fragrant	Mildews slightly	15-20'	General	Is rated as best climbing rose in most regions. Grows well and repeats blooming freely.
CLG. PEACE	Yellow bordered pink	Some fragrance	Resistant	15-20'	General	When it attains its mature growth, it is a wonderful climber producing the characteristically large Peace flowers in great profusion. A gorgeous sight against a dark wall.
CLG. PICTURE	Pink	Slight fragrance	Some mildew	8-15'	South and west	A splendid flower that grows vigorously, blooms freely, repeats well. Same flowers as the bush type, excellent for cutting.
CLG. TALISMAN	Yellow shaded cerise	Slight fragrance	Mildews	15-20'	South and west	Many prefer it to the bush type. A rank grower. Produces great quantity of blooms and repeats freely.
CLG. TEXAS CENTENNIAL	Light red	Very fragrant	Mildews slightly	15-20'	South and west	A worthy sport of President Hoover. Grows vigorously, and produces lovely, long-stemmed blooms in profusion. A very satisfactory climber.
GLADIATOR	Rose-red	Delicate fragrance	Resistant	8-10'	General	Pillar type. A hardy plant, blooming almost continuously over a long period. Large blooms of hybrid tea quality.
HIGH NOON (AARS)	Yellow	Slight fragrance	Very resistant	8-12'	General	Classed as a pillar type (8 feet), but in mild areas it often grows to three times that height.
MERMAID	Pale yellow	No fragrance	Very resistant	15-20'	General	Great vigor. Can be grown as a climber covering large areas, or as a hillside ground cover. Blooms continuously with large, single flowers.
PAUL'S SCARLET	Scarlet	Slight fragrance	Mildews slightly	10-15'	General	An ever-popular natural climber. Grows vigorously, producing many large clusters of blooms. Usually repeats if cut back after flowering.

QUEEN ELIZABETH
(grandiflora)

GOLDEN GIRL
(grandiflora)

MONTEZUMA
(grandiflora)

STARFIRE
(grandiflora)

18

FUSILIER
(floribunda)

MA PERKINS
(floribunda)

19

FIRE KING
(floribunda)

CIRCUS
(floribunda)

20

TAPESTRY
(hybrid tea)

HELEN TRAUBEL
(hybrid tea)

TANYA
(hybrid tea)

21

CHARLOTTE ARMSTRONG
(hybrid tea)

FIRST LOVE
(hybrid tea)

CHRYSLER IMPERIAL
(hybrid tea)

MOJAVE
(hybrid tea)

GAIL BORDEN
(hybrid tea)

23

STERLING SILVER
(hybrid tea)

GARDEN PARTY
(hybrid tea)

WHITE KNIGHT
(hybrid tea)

(Continued from page 10): Typical varieties are BLOOMFIELD COURAGE and LITTLE COMPTON CREEPER.

Actually, almost any climber can be trained as a ground cover by pegging it down. Roses like PEACE, TALLYHO, CHARLOTTE ARMSTRONG have been successfully used in this manner. When planting vigorous climbers for ground cover, the plants should be well spaced (20 feet apart). About 3 years should be allowed for coverage.

SHRUB ROSES

So-called "shrub" roses are mostly wild species, hybrids, and varieties that grow in an open, bush-like form. The most common representative of this class is *Rosa multiflora,* which is widely advertised. Shrub types are almost exclusively used for hedges, screen plantings, or game covers. Because they grow with great vigor, they are seldom planted outside rural areas where they can be given plenty of elbow room. A *Rosa multiflora* hedge, if left to its own devices, may cover a 15-foot swath. Pruning a well developed shrub rose calls for stout leather gauntlets— and considerable courage. The multiflora forms such a dense thicket that it is being tested by highway engineers as a traffic barrier to restrain cars that are forced off the road. Tests have proved that such a hedge can stop an automobile traveling 30 miles an hour in 24 feet. One Northwest landowner has found that his young multiflora hedge is better than barbed wire in keeping out pheasant hunters.

A hedge of multifloras can be maintained in a city garden provided it is clipped three or four times a year. Clipping removes the new growth that produces flowers, but enough are likely to remain to produce bright fruits, or hips that may remain far into winter. In mild areas, multifloras will retain their foliage through the winter.

Most of the shrub types produce a profusion of small, delicate blooms that are not only difficult to pick without personal scars, but which fall apart at a touch.

MINIATURE ROSES

How do you look at a miniature rose? Whether you have eyes for its intriguing duplication on a miniature scale of leaf, thorn, bud, and flower of the standard rose, or for its compact form as a small shrub, will determine the use you make of it. As an intriguing novelty in a 4 or 6-inch pot, to be viewed at less than arm's length, it has limited use and is somewhat of a chore to keep. However, as a small, hardy shrub it has a certain place in the garden, particularly in the rock garden section.

These are true roses with miniature canes, foliage, and flowers. Normally they grow to a height of 6 to 12 inches and bear flowers from $\frac{1}{2}$ to 1 inch in diameter. They bear their flowers in masses and bloom throughout spring and summer months. They are closely related to the *Rosa chinensis.*

Miniatures are becoming popular in many areas, not in the sense of garden roses with a wide range of usefulness in garden and lawn areas, but as a novel plant for rock gardens, miniature collections, doll house gardens, window boxes, and specimen pot plants.

Miniatures also have a limited use as borders and edgings. They have several shortcomings as border plants. They demand constant care and are easily damaged. The individual plants are relatively expensive, and because they must be planted close together to produce a border, their aggregate cost for a border planting is usually disproportionate to their performance.

If you are attracted to miniature roses, you are well advised to try one or two in your garden before launching a large collection.

Culture Indoors and Out

Miniatures require careful cultural attention, different from that accorded to full-size roses. They have tiny, shallow roots, and as a consequence the soil around the plants must be kept moist at all times, usually by light daily watering in most localities. They should be fed moderately if their dwarf characteristics are to be retained. Use liquid fertilizer at about half the strength recommended for full-size rose plants. Feed monthly during the growing season.

Prune lightly to shape the plants. Cut off faded blossoms and dead wood. Cut back any shoots that extend beyond the foliage. Some successful growers cut back the plant to 1 inch above the soil surface just before the start of the growing season and so produce entirely fresh plant growth.

Although most miniatures are quite hardy, they should be well covered with protective materials in severe-winter areas.

For use as potted plants, set miniatures in 6-inch pots filled with rich garden loam. In a smaller pot, they will dry out too rapidly. As pot plants, they can be kept indoors, but they will not thrive in a dry, warm, close room. They do not relish the air in a gas-heated house. To provide the necessary rest period, put pots in frost-free storage from late fall until January. Then, place them in a sunny window and feed monthly with a weak liquid fertilizer. They can be set outdoors in April or May.

Propagation

Cuttings of miniature roses are very easy to start, especially in midsummer while the wood is firm but still growing. Start in flats in wet sand in the greenhouse, in a cold-frame, or in a protected shady place in the garden.

Varieties

The following plants are recommended:

TOM THUMB—perfect form, probably the smallest of the miniatures; deep crimson with white eye; double.

ROULETTI *(Rosa chinensis minima)*—double light pink; oldest variety.

PIXIE—most double (40 petals); flushed pink, but blush pink in cold weather.

WHITE FAIRY—white tinged with pink in cool weather; in clusters; double.

BABY GOLD STAR—golden yellow.

PYGMY GOLD—golden yellow clusters.

BO PEEP—deep rose pink; double.

SWEET FAIRY—dark pink buds open to apple blossom pink; double.

PINK MIDGET—clear medium pink; double.

MIDGET—rose red; very double.

PYGMY RED—dark red with tiny white eye.

RED ELF—double; darkest velvety red, white eye.

OLD-FASHIONED ROSES

A collector of "old-fashioned" roses is usually a gardener who is surfeited with the moderns. He may be horticulturally inclined and collect the wild or species roses from which the modern roses are descended. He may be a sentimentalist and gather the roses of historical significance. Or he may just prefer the simple beauty of the single blossom or the fragrance of its foliage after a rain. An increasing interest in old-fashioned roses has encouraged specialists to grow them. Some noteworthy varieties are still obtainable—but not always with ease. Most of them can only be secured from the few nurseries that specialize in them.

Tea Roses

Tea roses, ancestor of the hybrid teas, are vigorous and everblooming, and, like their famous descendants, produce large, attractive flowers. Petal substance is inferior, however, and flower necks are weak, causing flowers to droop. Tea roses, too, are much less hardy than hybrid teas.

Hybrid Perpetuals

The hybrid perpetuals dominated the rose scene from 1840 to 1890, when they were superseded by their offspring, the hybrid teas. One reason for their decline was that the flower of many perpetuals does not bear the popular, long-pointed bud of the hybrid tea and, generally speaking, the plant blooms less frequently in summer. They are tall, vigorous growers so should be planted behind lower growing roses. Hybrid perpetuals are still popular in cold sections because of their superior hardiness.

FRAU KARL DRUSCHKI is the only hybrid perpetual which has firmly held its ground. It still ranks high in the white rose class. The 5 to 6-foot bush has large foliage and is covered with pure white flowers which look very much like camellias.

The Briers

The so-called Austrian briers which came from Asia carry the botanical name *R. foetida.* The flower has a sharp, almost musky fragrance. The briers are tall shrubs, from 6 to 10 feet high, and all wear an unusual, lacy, fern-like foliage. Since they lose bloom by pruning, they are often set out in alternate plantings to allow a complete cutback every 3 or 4 years without loss of garden color.

HARISON'S YELLOW, developed in America in 1830, is a hybrid that was rapidly accepted in our gardens. It was packed westward in many pioneer wagons and can be seen today in the ghost towns of the gold country. This rose was often used as a large, 6-foot shrub to give the garden a blaze of yellow color following forsythia. In the Pacific Northwest, pioneers frequently planted it with a clump of old-fashioned blue lilac.

Giganteas

The most famous of these roses, BELLE OF PORTUGAL, is still widely sold and planted. Like the teas, it's a tender rose and will freeze down in cool areas, but where the weather is warm, BELLE will smother the house. The Willamette Valley in Oregon knows BELLE OF PORTUGAL as "the mission rose" because of a well known planting around one of the first religious establishments there.

Other Old Types

The Noisettes, the moss roses, and other old-fashioned roses like the bourbons, damasks, chinas, cabbage roses, and others, may be of sentimental interest to collectors but are generally inferior to modern roses.

The Noisette rose, MARECHAL NIEL, a yellow climber, is still considered a superb rose. ROSE OF CASTILE, a hardy, pest-resistant damask rose came to California with the padres and lived on in some missions to hide crumbling adobe walls. Its flowers are double, soft deep pink, and fragrant.

The floribunda rose, MARGO KOSTER, *bloomed in* Sun*set gardens in Menlo Park from May to mid-December*

Pillar-type rose, GLADIATOR, *has large blooms of hybrid tea type. Foliage is dark green, large, decorative*

WHICH ROSES ARE THE MOST FRAGRANT?

One of the most charming attributes that a rose may have is fragrance.

We say "may have" because many very beautiful roses have little or no discernible fragrance.

The sweet scent of a rose has an evanescent charm difficult to describe or classify. That of any variety may vary in strength and type at different hours of the day. It is affected by temperature and degrees of humidity, by sunlight, and by shade. These scents develop best in a warm, humid atmosphere and are retarded by cool, wet, or very dry conditions.

The odorous oils of roses are of a very complex nature, each variety being made up of many different alcohol esters and aldehydes of a volatile type. They are found chiefly in the flower and its component parts, but their fragrance can often be noted in the leaves, roots and bark.

Rose perfumes, being indefinite and variable, are most difficult to describe; hence, there is no practical or scientific basis for classifying them. Most rose fanciers define them by their resemblance to the real or imagined fragrance of other flowers, fruits, or shrubs. More than fifty such name comparisons have been noted in book and catalog descriptions. For instance, rose scents are likened to the fragrance of apple, apricot, almond, peach, tangerine, orange, muscat grape, nuts, spices, tea, honey.

Are Old Roses More Fragrant Than New?

Are the old roses more fragrant than the new varieties of today? This query is always a subject for debate among rose growers, particularly those whose rose education started some time ago.

It is true that many of the best modern varieties have little or no fragrance; however, be assured that the same proportion of the old-time roses had a similar lack of perfume.

In the spring of 1950, Dr. Walter Lammerts, an eminent hybridizer and rose authority, conducted an interesting experiment. He, with a group of other rose experts, made an organized test of the fragrance characteristics of a great many varieties in the Descanso Rose History Gardens in Southern California. This garden contains some 600 varieties of roses, including nearly every important variety introduced from about the year 1500 to the present time.

The most important varieties of each period of rose history were tested for fragrance by the different members of the committee of experts. The conclusions arrived at by the panel surprised even the authorities themselves.

Their findings toppled the old belief that all old roses are fragrant. The test proved rather conclusively that since the beginning of rose history, only about one-third of the varieties introduced in each period could be classified as "fragrant" to "very-fragrant." About the same proportion would classify as "moderately fragrant," and a like proportion as having little or no fragrance.

The panel discovered that few of the more fragrant old-time roses equalled the intensity and variety of fragrance given off by such modern roses as MIRANDY, MISS CLIPPER, HEART'S DESIRE, SUTTER'S GOLD, SAN FERNANDO, or TALLYHO.

In one sense, it is remarkable that today's hybridizers are maintaining just as high a percentage of fragrant varieties as the breeders of the past, because modern hybridizers consider fragrance a desirable but not essential characteristic. When they are developing a new rose, they breed primarily for perfection of color, blossom form, and vigor of growth. Fragrance is rated as a recessive factor, a weak characteristic that is liable to disappear in the hybrids.

Intensely fragrant varieties, if crossed, will usually yield a high percentage of fragrant seedlings. The rich velvety crimsons such as MIRANDY, ETOILE DE HOLLANDE, CRIMSON GLORY, and CHARLES MALLERIN, can always be expected to emit a heady perfume inherited from a far-away damask ancestor. Roses of a pink blend can be expected to inherit fragrance from the same sources as the deep reds—the damasks and the centifolias—but to a lesser degree of intensity. Notably fragrant pinks: DAME EDITH HELEN, HECTOR DEANE, LA FRANCE, and MISS CLIPPER.

On the other hand, the brilliant scarlets, such as POINSETTIA and SOUTHPORT, do not seem to benefit from their inheritance. Likewise, the pure yellow varieties can rarely be rated as fragrant. When yellows are intensely fragrant, like SUTTER'S GOLD, they show some diffusion of red coloring.

Certain rose parents are favored because they consistently introduce fragrance into their seedlings and their offspring. Three such parents are OPHELIA, HOOSIER BEAUTY, and PREMIER.

If you desire to plant varieties of fine fragrance in your garden, here is a list to choose from:

HECTOR DEANE	CAPISTRANO
GIRONA	NEIGE PARFUM
MIRANDY (not for coastal areas)	TAWNY GOLD
	ETOILE DE HOLLANDE
HEART'S DESIRE	POLLY
SUTTER'S GOLD	SHOT SILK
SAN FERNANDO	ANGEL'S MATEU
MISS CLIPPER	CHARLES MALLERIN
TALLYHO	TEXAS CENTENNIAL
CRIMSON GLORY	IMPERIAL POTENTATE
PRES. HERBERT HOOVER	THE DOCTOR
CHRYSLER IMPERIAL	TIFFANY

CHAPTER THREE

How to Buy Rose Plants

When purchasing rose plants, you will be wise to remember that you are investing in a plant that should serve you well for fifteen years or more. A little extra time, a bit more care in selection, perhaps an additional dollar or two spent at the time you choose your rose bushes will well repay you over the years.

WAYS OF BUYING ROSES

Roses are sold in four forms:

1. Bare-root bushes in nursery bins.

2. Bare-root bushes shipped by mail from mail-order nurseries.

3. Packaged and wrapped bare-root plants sold in department stores and chain stores.

4. Plants in containers.

Each of these methods of sale has its advantages—and its disadvantages.

BUYING FROM THE NURSERY BIN

Many rose growers consider the best way to buy roses is to buy bare-root stock at the nursery. These plants are stored in open bins during the dormant period, their roots buried in damp sawdust, sand, or other material.

Buying bushes in this manner gives you the opportunity to pick out top quality stock for your garden. Choose plants that have plump, green canes with smooth, unshriveled bark, and a good well balanced root system. Roots and tops should have a fresh appearance. A bush in good condition will have weight; a dried-out bush will be abnormally light and brittle.

A reliable nurseryman will guarantee that his roses will grow well and bloom, if properly handled and planted. Although most nurserymen are more than fair in replacing bushes, they confess that most of the plant failures are due to mistakes made by the purchaser. To be fair to your dealer, follow the planting directions carefully and give the plant ample time to make good before asking for a replacement. (See information on this subject in the planting chapter.)

BUYING ROSES BY MAIL

For many gardeners, ordering roses from a catalog has advantages over picking them out of the nursery bins. The choice of available varieties is usually much wider. Only a few of the larger nurseries can afford to keep a large assortment of rose varieties in stock. New introductions can often be obtained more quickly, from mail-order dealers. Furthermore, in some localities, the nearest nursery is several miles away and it is thus more convenient to shop by mail, particularly during the winter months when driving is no pleasure.

At the drop of a postcard, you can obtain excellent catalogs, blazing with color. The rose blooms are reproduced as accurately as modern printing processes permit. In addition, the catalogs provide useful information about growing habits. However, the beginner needs some guidance in finding his way through these beautiful pages.

How to "Expert" the Catalogs

Anyone who has dreamed through several rose catalogs is bound to conclude that there is no such thing as a poor rose. All the varieties shown in their vibrant color are extolled in glowing terms. As a matter of fact, these superlatives are not so far from the truth as they may seem to a cynical reader. Plants sold by mail by reliable rose dealers are, in general, tops in quality and they should develop into the perfection shown in the catalog, if grown under proper conditions.

There is a "catch," though—and a big catch it is, too. Although a particular catalog may not indicate any limitations, not every rose listed in it will perform well in every garden. Roses will grow almost anywhere—the national scope of the mail-order rose business is evidence of this

—but some roses do better than others in different climates. A couple of dozen varieties or more will perform capably in any climate, but the majority show definite preferences.

One rose may bloom profusely in a hot climate and open sparingly in a cool or foggy area. Another one may ball up and burn in heat.

The way to use the handsome catalog, then, is to find out for yourself which of these queenly plants will do well in your garden. Pick out the ones that interest you, then check your list this way:

1. Match it against the recommended varieties charted in this book.

2. Check your list against the name tags in your municipal rose garden, if you have one.

3. Talk to the rose enthusiasts in your neighborhood; visit their gardens. Find out which of the varieties they are growing do well.

4. Write to the American Rose Society for a copy of their rating list and guide to purchasing roses.

5. Check your selections against the climate column in the chart on pages 12 to 16.

6. It is of utmost importance to get your rose orders in early, preferably in the early fall. Specify an early delivery date giving careful consideration to the time when you expect to do your planting.

It is well to give a second choice when placing late orders. It is better to specify any substitute you will accept than to leave the choice to the seller. Otherwise you are apt to receive some variety you already have or do not want.

HOW TO BUY PACKAGED ROSES

Every year during the rose planting seasons, packaged roses appear in quantity on the counters of five-and-ten cent stores, drug stores, department stores, and supermarkets. Often, these plants are priced at an attractively low level.

Now, it is quite possible to purchase a good rose in this manner, but as a general rule, the odds are against your getting a genuine bargain of a desirable rose.

The reasons are simple: Few stores that are not designed for handling plant materials provide the right environment for rose bushes. Department stores or chain stores, for instance, are usually over-heated throughout the winter months, and some of them are kept warm even when closed at night and over weekends. This cozy warmth that feels so welcome to the shopper escaping the cold blasts outdoors, is tough on dormant roses. The

bushes may either be forced into premature growth by the unseasonal heat or dried out by the over-heated air.

In some stores, a conscientious effort is made to protect the bushes, and if you have such a dealer in your locality, you may be able to get good results from the stock he offers.

So-called "bargain" roses, offered at ridiculously low prices, should be approached with great caution. These plants may be culls from a growing field, of little value; they may be distress stock from a nursery that was unable to dispose of its entire allotment before growth started; or they may be cast-offs from the commercial rose trade, greenhouse roses discarded after their third and last season of production.

Unfortunately, the policing of merchandising practices of this character is lax in many states, so the risk is all on the side of the rose purchaser. Sometimes you can find top quality stock of unpatented roses offered in this manner, and if the plants meet the standards set forth above, and if the firm is known to be reliable, you can probably buy with confidence.

HOW TO BUY ROSES IN CONTAINERS

Because of many practical advantages offered, many gardeners like the idea of planting roses from 3 and 5-gallon cans and other containers. As a consequence, you will find many nurseries featuring roses in containers during the late spring and summer months.

Advantages of Container Roses

Plantings can be made at late dates when bare-root roses are unobtainable.

Growing plants can be procured to replace dead or undesirable bushes and to fill in occasionally bare spots. In late spring these container plants should be in bloom and the purchaser can study the growing habits, foliage and flower of various types and varieties to better aid in making his choice.

(NOTE: The ultimate growing height of any variety will not be shown by the early growth of these container plants. For height information refer to the charts on pages 12 to 16.)

Some nurseries make a specialty of container roses. They bring them along with care to have them ready after the bare-root season ends. Many buy stocks especially for container planting and do not can any but the best of the early season's carry-over. If your nursery follows such excellent practices, you can feel safe in buying from it.

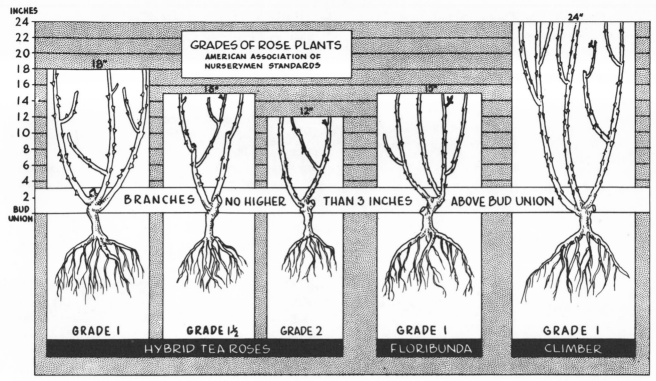

Disadvantages

The roots being concealed, the purchaser cannot detect a poor or diseased root system or one that has been badly cut or broken off in harvesting or handling.

Many container roses are supplied from the nursery's surplus left over at the end of the season after the better and larger bushes have been picked out. Choice of varieties is usually limited in these end-of-season stocks, the season's best sellers having been sold out.

Container stocks cannot be shipped by parcel post. They are bulky and heavy and, consequently, are expensive to crate and ship by any means. Most dealers will not ship.

There is a tendency for some dealers to get rid of inferior plants by canning them rather than to take a loss by destroying them. This is particularly true of the more costly patent varieties. Container roses are usually priced at a small advance of 25c to 50c over bare-root stock.

Tips on Buying

1. Avoid roses planted in 1-gallon cans or small flower pots. Small containers do not provide sufficient room for root growth.

2. Buy your rose in the largest container offered. Three or 5-gallon sizes are probably the best, but 10-inch tar-paper pots can support good stock.

3. If you have the choice, buy only No. 1 roses (see details below). You may get a good buy in 1½ grade in the smaller varieties, but it will pay you to accept only the best in case the bush has been at all handicapped by being raised in a container.

4. Buy bushes that were planted the same year. Avoid plants that have been carried over from the previous year —their roots are liable to be restricted. Tell-tale signs of holdover stock are pruning scars from the previous season, dead wood, or a snaggle of small branches resulting from lack of pruning.

5. Buy your plants before the heat of summer has taken hold. Roses kept in cans through a hot summer usually suffer from lack of water or fertilizer or from root tips burned from touching the hot metal sides of the container.

ROSE GRADING SYSTEM

The rose you buy is graded under a standard established by the American Association of Nurserymen system, e.g.:

No. 1 Grade Hybrid Tea and Grandiflora

Three or more strong canes, two of which are to be 18 inches long and up before cutting back by the seller, with the exception of some of the light-growing varieties, which are to have three canes (or more), two of which are to be 16 inches and up, one cane to be 18 inches, branched not more than 3 inches above the bud union.

No. 1½ Grade Hybrid Tea and Grandiflora

Two or more strong canes, to be 15 inches and up with the exception of some of the light-growing varieties which must have two strong canes 13 inches and up, and branched not higher than 3 inches above the bud union.

No. 2 Grade Hybrid Tea and Grandiflora

Two or more strong canes 12 inches and up, with the exception of light-growing varieties which must have two canes 10 inches and up.

No. 1 Grade Floribundas

Three or more strong canes, two of which must be 15 inches and up, with exception of light-growing varieties which must have three canes 13 inches and up, branched not more than 3 inches above the bud union.

No. 1½ Grade Floribundas

Two canes 14 inches and up, lighter varieties 12 inches and up.

No. 1 Grade Polyantha

Four or more canes 12 inches and up. No. 2 grade of no value.

No. 1 Grade Climbers

Three or more canes 24 inches and up, except *R. wichuraianas* No. 1½ grade which must have two canes 18 inches and up.

You're wisest to insist on No. 1 or 1½ grade, either of which will develop into a good plant. With No. 2 plants, you're starting out with a handicap.

Plants should be two-year-old, field-grown stock in dormant stage, but in fresh condition, root and top.

Often the nurseryman will have cut all the canes back to 12 or 14 inches and will have trimmed back the roots. This reduces the shipping weight and permits the plants to be expressed in smaller cartons. If the cut-back canes and roots are of good quality and caliber and the root development well balanced, these bushes should be accepted as No. 1 or 1½ grade if so labeled. The cut-back has usually readied them for planting.

Note that specifications for the size of new bushes differ with the various varieties, and this must be taken into consideration when you make your selection. For example, "Two-year-old" bushes of such top varieties as Mrs. Sam McGredy, Christopher Stone, Snowbird and some others may be small in comparison with such vigorous varieties as Peace, President Hoover, or Signora. Rarely do two different varieties grow exactly alike.

PATENTS VS. NON-PATENTS

A tag on a rose plant indicating that it is a patented variety has no bearing on its quality or beauty. The patent merely reserves the growing rights to the originator or licensee, and the owner retains the privilege of setting the same price throughout the country.

Many patented roses are excellent, proven varieties. Virtually all of the recently introduced hybrid teas carry patent tags. But some patented roses have proven to be unsatisfactory under specific growing conditions. Some of the finest roses in the nursery bins do not carry the little metal patent tag.

ALL-AMERICA ROSE SELECTIONS

The All-America symbol (A.A.R.S.), on the other hand, means a great deal. Some of the very finest offerings of the rose world, from Europe as well as the United States, carry the A.A.R.S. brand.

It indicates that the rose has been observed for two seasons and found to be a superior variety in the 22 official trial gardens authorized by All-America Rose Selections, an organization of introducers and commercial growers. In these gardens, expert rosarians try out a great many new roses entered for trial by rose hybridizers and producers. The new roses are rated impartially on a point basis and each year the one or two that pass the extremely strict tests are announced early in the following year. So high are the standards of the All-America selectors that no roses were accepted as worthy of the A.A.R.S. symbol in 1951 and no hybrid tea roses in 1954.

AMERICAN ROSE SOCIETY RATINGS

As a further check on the quality of rose plants on the market, the American Rose Society conducts its own rating service. It publishes an annual buying guide based on accumulated reports from hundreds of members in this country and Canada. Hybrid tea, floribunda, grandiflora and climber classes are rated on a scale of 10. A national rating of 10 is a perfect rose (none has made it yet); from 9 to 9.9 are outstanding varieties; from 8 to 8.9 are excellent roses; from 7 to 7.9 are good; and from 6 to 6.9 are fair. Any ratings lower than 6 represent varieties of questionable value. However, some roses with low ratings have individual characteristics that make them desirable for certain garden situations.

For the complete listing of modern roses and their ratings, revised annually, you can write to the American Rose Society, 4048 Roselea Place, Columbus 14, Ohio. In addition to ratings, the listing indicates relative height, relative fragrance, and color of each rose.

CHAPTER FOUR

How to Use Roses in Your Garden

Not too many years ago, the man who wanted to specialize in growing roses displayed his plants in marshaled beds, bisected and intersected with neat paths converging on a bird bath, a sundial, or a treillage. Even in small gardens, rose fanciers attempted to carry forward landscaping fashions that were established when the rose was a court favorite and rose gardens were laid out in royal estates.

In recent years, landscaping emphasis has shifted away from gardens-to-look-at to gardens-to-live-in. The dimensions of many of today's gardens are measured to fit people—as well as plants. Members of the family are learning to treat their outdoor space like an extension of their indoor living; and not many families are willing to give over an entire yard to rose growing, for there are other diversions that compete for the space—outdoor cooking, dining and entertaining, children's play, or space for just relaxing.

This shift in family interest has seen a parallel change in rose styles and landscaping uses. The developing popularity of the floribunda, with its easy maintenance and its effective massed color, probably reflects to some extent the desire of many gardeners to possess this matchless flower without in turn being possessed by it. Although the very striking and individualistic hybrid teas still account for the bulk of the rose sales, even these plants lend themselves to incidental use in a lived-in garden—pillars against a fence, bushes along the driveway, standards in a border, climbers smothering a fence around a pool. With their matchless color, form, and fragrance, roses bring a gracious element into a modern garden plan and provide a good solid link with the gardens of the past.

Of course, not everyone fully accepts the doctrines of indoor-outdoor living, and there are many formal rose gardens being planted today. For some gardeners, this seems a truer setting for the rose than incidental placement in a modern plan. The formal garden has a long and respected tradition behind it that recognizes the formal and austere side of the rose. Many rosarians feel that when the rose is grown with understanding and proper care, it is best set apart by itself, aloof from other shrubs and flowering plants. On the practical side, roses do benefit from being isolated—their cultural needs differ from other plants, they need lots of space for good air circulation and proper exposure to the sun, and they do better when their roots do not have to compete for food.

Where and how you use roses in your own garden are problems that you alone can solve. If you need only a single climber to cover a single trellis, a half dozen standards to line your entryway, a selection of hybrid teas for a cutting garden, or a forest of rose bushes, you can gain ideas from seeing how others have used roses in a similar fashion; but the final decision on placement and design is yours, because no one book can tell you everything you need to know.

In this chapter, you will find ideas for using roses. The photographs display roses in garden settings. In some cases they are used as simple, informal additions to the modern garden; in other examples they are given prominence as the featured plant in the garden. Some of these gardens are owner-planned; some are professionally designed.

REQUIREMENTS FOR ROSE PLANTING

Before you get too deep into planning your rose garden, you should check your desires against the limitations that roses set for themselves.

1. Roses should be planted to remain in a permanent location, because they do not relish being disturbed.

2. Roses should receive a maximum of direct sunlight. Six hours a day—preferably in the morning—will give excellent results. In a very cool climate, dawn-to-dusk sunlight will do no harm—in fact, it will encourage vigorous growth and prolific bloom.

3. Avoid continuous shade, particularly from directly overhead. Roses will grow in the shade, but they will grow rank and produce scant bloom.

The control of mildew and rust is much more difficult in the shade. In localities with searing heat, however, the rose plants should be partially shaded from the intense glare of the afternoon sun.

4. Avoid planting in a windy area. A free circulation of air is desirable for plant health, but a strong or continuous wind will damage the blooms.

5. Although rich soil is very desirable, any fairly good loam can be modified and improved by the addition of humus-building materials and soil correctives.

6. You must provide good drainage, because roses will never thrive with "wet feet." If necessary, plan for raised beds to insure proper drainage.

7. Avoid planting within range of the roots of trees and shrubs, which will be certain to steal food and moisture from the root system of your roses.

8. If possible, allow ground room for expansion of your plantings. Once you have started a rose garden, you are likely to add to it as each new spring brings forth irresistible new rose varieties. If you do not wish to complete your garden in the first year, plan for step-by-step development over a two or three-year period.

9. Consider the view of the rose garden from fortunately located windows. Bring the garden into your home through the windows.

10. On the other hand, don't forget that the rose is deciduous and not at its prettiest in its leafless state. Use low evergreens in the foreground or tall ones in the background to attract the eye when the rose plants are leafless.

HOW MANY PLANTS?

The spacing of rose bushes depends upon the locality where grown and the varieties being planted.

In areas with a long growing season, such as prevails in the West and South, rose bushes attain much greater size than in areas with heavy frosts and a brief growing season.

Throughout most of the Pacific Coast, the South, and the Southwest, hybrid teas and grandifloras are normally planted 24 to 36 inches apart from one bud union to another. Within these regions are local areas with exceptionally favorable growing conditions where rose bushes grow so prodigiously that they must be planted 36 to 48 inches apart.

Floribundas are planted closer together, usually 18 to 24 inches apart, except for a few sprawlers such as GOLDILOCKS which require more space.

Planting to the minimum figures mentioned above conserves space for gardens with limited area. It also provides a pleasing view of flowers and green top foliage instead of exposed soil and brown canes.

SUGGESTED COLOR COMBINATIONS

There are innumerable rules for blending colors in the garden, but the rose grower who sensibly avoids color clashes—such as a blue-red climber against an orange-red brick wall—can generally create pleasing effects by following simple recommendations like these:

1. Keep roses of the same or related hues massed together instead of mixing colors in a hodgepodge.

2. To make a bed appear deeper than it is, place light tones in the back, dark in front. To foreshorten, reverse the order.

3. For effective display, check anticipated height of growth when you buy plants, so you can set them out with no fear of their obscuring other rose bushes.

4. To accent rose color, combine rose plantings with other flowering plants, or match them with house or fence colors. Here are some suggestions:

Roses Against Architectural Color

The striking red climbers, BLAZE or PAUL'S SCARLET, against a wall of gray or white. A beautiful red NEW YORKER against white or light green. That finest of climbers, MRS. SAM MCGREDY, with its coppery pinks against a warm gray or natural redwood. The fiery scarlet floribunda, SIREN, massed as a foundation planting for a white house. A thick hedge of the rich pink floribunda, FROLIC, with a blue or gray house trim. The brilliant yellow climber, SUNGOLD, against a warm gray wall.

Rose Colors Blended with Perennial Blooms

The striking CHRYSLER IMPERIAL with true blue delphiniums in the background. PINKIE as a low hedge with blue violas. Pink POULSEN'S BEDDER with a border of ageratum. A hedge of the lovely floribunda, ROSENELFE, behind a border of light blue lobelias. Pink floribunda, LILIBET, climbing with lavendar-blue clematis.

Roses with Bulbs

Yellow ECLIPSE and GOLDEN SCEPTER with dark purple iris. CHARLOTTE ARMSTRONG or CAPISTRANO with Regal lilies. The glowing orange MOJAVE combined with brown-toned iris. Brilliant orange-red floribunda, CINNABAR, is striking with white iris.

Roses are planted on upper level of garden (see plan below). Two levels separated by slope covered with spring bulbs, summer annuals. Gray-green wall provides privacy, protects plants from cold-season winds

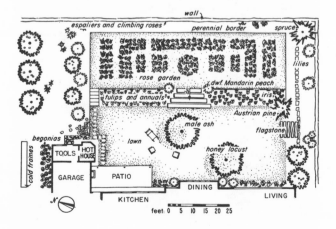

RIGHT

With imaginative design, roses can be dramatically used to enrich the garden. Here, two colors of floribundas are blended in raised bed walled with used brick. Tree is Modesto ash. Designer: Thomas Church

Tree roses rimming this semi-circular driveway provide colorful welcome to visitors. Clipped privet and low-growing floribundas make an attractive base planting

Three tree roses, with base planting of clipped privet and dwarf cotoneaster, provide an effective, decorative separation between this entrance walk and drive

The floribunda rose, REDCAP, is used effectively here as a hedge to separate wide driveway from lawn area, adding color and breaking expanse of lawn and pavement

This long parking strip is attractively planted with a row of standard roses. Tamarisk juniper and rose-colored fibrous begonias are used as effective base planting

Hybrid tea roses planted against baffle fence provide colorful background for plants in this raised bed at edge of lawn area. Designers: Osmundson and Staley

The floribunda rose, CIRCUS, decorates side of graveled patio. Angled design of rose beds adds interest to the patio and gives ample planting space for the rose bushes

The floribunda rose, FASHION, is used here as a low-growing border plant to provide a touch of bright color next to wall at the edge of this garden pool

Hybrid tea roses with a background of espaliered pears highlight alternate panels of fence to give interesting pattern to garden. Designers: Osmundson and Staley

Floribundas in raised bed provide bright spot of color in this patio. The used-brick walls of the plant bed | *blend with the patio paving. Note weep holes in raised bed to provide drainage. Designer: Lockwood deForest*

Compact, low-growing roses can be used very effectively in border plantings. The rose growing in front of this picket fence is pink floribunda, CHINA DOLL

Hedges of floribunda rose, FASHION, line the sides of paved walk leading to house, accentuate long, graceful curve of walk and break up the wide sweep of lawn

A single variety of white floribunda rose graces this handsome foundation planting against the used-brick walls of the house. The planting extends beyond end of house to form a hedge. Designer: Thomas Church

Box at right has a raised cap to allow trailing plants at base of the roses to grow through the opening and spill over edges of the box. Photo above shows detail of rose beds. Beds are edged with 2 by 6-inch headers

Pillar roses are grown effectively in panels against grapestake fence. Each rose is trained on a fence-high stake. Planting in the foreground is sedum; trees behind the fence are hawthorns. Designer: Jack Gibson

EGLANTINE rose is planted on fence near path where its sweet, apple-scented fragrance can be enjoyed by the passerby. The leaves are pleasantly fragrant when wet

Trellis-fence built around this patio supports climbing roses planted in redwood boxes. Smooth rocks cover soil in raised bed. Designers: Litton and Whitney

Climber, HIGH NOON, *trained on wall in sight of living room windows. Free-form bed contains evergreens*

Climbing rose on trellis fastened to the overhang of this storage shed permits easy repainting of wall behind

Delicate tracery of small-foliaged yellow climbing rose is effective against the gray-green walls of this house

MRS. SAM McGREDY, *grown on rail fence in front Sunset building, draws comment because of prolific bloom*

Climbing roses are trained to cover a board fence. Rose pictured, CLIMBING PEACE, *is about five years old*

This traditional use of PAUL'S SCARLET *climbing rose on picket fence harmonizes with Western ranch house*

41

Rose gardens for the lover of roses do not always have to be laid out in strictly formal shapes, as this garden demonstrates. The five beds in the foreground are edged with privet. Four tree roses grow in the lawn, beds of hybrid teas in background beyond lawn. Paths are rough-troweled concrete. Beds are large enough to permit easy culture of roses. *Designer: Thomas Church*

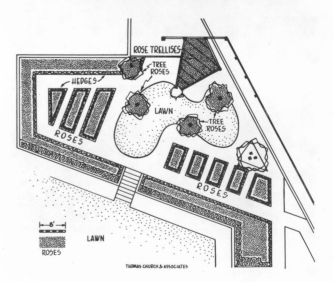

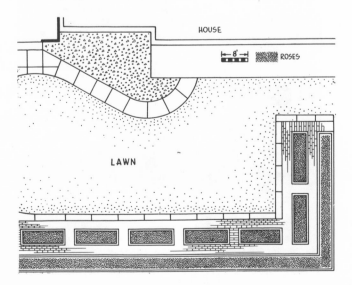

Tailored beds are used in this modern rose garden to display roses to best advantage. A raised bed runs along fence parallel to the seven island beds (see plan). Headers formed of 2 by 10-inch redwood are capped with mitered 2 by 6's. Evergreen pears are espaliered on fence in background. Designer: Thomas Church

The orange-buff and pink shades of the floribunda rose, CIRCUS, give a pleasing display of color in planting bed between paved floor of patio and brick wall behind

Tall-growing grandiflora rose, ROUNDELAY, provides interesting contrast in height and color when planted behind the lower growing, compact polyantha, PINKIE

Three-year-old multiflora hedge was planted to shield house from the road. Hedge is now 5 feet high, 4 feet wide, 75 feet long, needs trimming three times a year

Clipped multiflora hedge in front garden bears white flowers in June and red berries until Christmas. Hedge prevents dogs and children from cutting across the lawn

CHAPTER FIVE

How to Plant Roses

One pleasant feature of the rose as a garden plant is its ease in planting. The procedure is not so simple as fitting a gallon-can earth ball into a post hole, but the mechanics of planting are simple and relatively standard. There are a few rules to follow to insure a successful planting, but it is hard to go wrong in setting out rose bushes.

Because 90 per cent of roses are still planted bare-root, the procedure below is confined to this method of planting. A separate section on planting from containers follows.

WHEN TO PLANT

Bare-root roses are planted during dormancy. Preferred times are after roses go dormant or shortly before the buds break.

The dormant period varies by climate. In mild-winter areas, it may be as short as a few weeks or a couple of months—in Hawaii roses do not go dormant at all. In severe-winter areas, the dormant period lasts four to six months.

In an area with a brief dormant period, the choice may be narrowed down to January-February. So it is that in much of California, the best time to plant is during a single brief period between January 1 and March 1; but in the mountain states, the Midwest, and East, where winters are long, there is a choice between fall and spring planting.

If necessary, the planting time in your locality can be extended 30 days if care is used to prevent drying out of the bushes before and after planting. Roots should be kept damp and the mounding up protection maintained.

Another factor in the determination of planting time is always the availability of the bushes you desire to plant. Most roses are harvested in late October, November, and early December. Sometimes excessive rains in the late autumn will delay harvesting and retard the marketing of rose bushes.

Chart of Planting Dates

Here are recommended times for planting bare-root roses in major climate zones:

Area	First choice	Second choice
Southern California	Jan-Feb	Spring
Northern California Coast	Dec 15-Mar 1	Mar 1-Apr 1*
Northern California Mountains	Mar 15-Apr 1*	
Central California and Bay Area	Dec 15-Mar 1	Spring*
Western Washington and Oregon	Fall	Spring*
Eastern Washington and Oregon	Fall	
Florida and Gulf States	Nov-Jan 15	
Middle Atlantic States	Fall	
Midwest	Fall	

*Depending on early spring temperatures, ground thaw, and availablity of rose planting stock.

Sometimes a plant will be slow in starting or developing after it has been planted. Some may remain green for a long time and still not break. This is not due to a defect or diseased condition in the rose; it merely means that a particular rose plant is a slowpoke, lazy in getting started. To prod it along, use the damp peat fence discussed below. This treatment will nearly always cause the laggard to catch up with the faster plantings by mid-season.

Fall vs. Spring Planting

Where the gardener is offered the choice between fall and spring planting, he will probably find opinion evenly balanced on the subject. Easiest way to decide is to follow the practice recommended locally by the majority of your nurserymen, park gardeners, or rosarians, always depending on the availability of rose bush supplies.

Here is a summary of the reasons offered for and against the two seasons:

Fall Planting: Bushes may be set out when the ground is still workable and the weather is pleasant. Plants will have time to establish root systems before the onset of spring growth.

Disadvantages: You will need to protect the canes against winter damage and you may lose plants in a severe freeze. In some localities, ground freezes early and roses set out in fall do not have time to develop any root growth before the freeze. On the other hand, a warm winter may break the buds prematurely and make the plant vulnerable to a spring frost.

Spring Planting: Considered by many authorities to be the safest time for planting in areas with very cold winters—provided the planting is done early in the spring. Availability of new stock is greater at this time, and some types of rose plants, notably tree roses, are available only in spring. Heavy protection of plants against freezing is not necessary.

Disadvantages: Sometimes the ground will not be workable until late in spring; or it may be cold even though the air is warm and balmy, thus retarding root growth at the same time that top growth is accelerated.

Container Plants

Roses bought in 5-gallon cans or in large tar-paper pots may be planted spring through summer. See section on page 50 on this type of planting.

PREPARING ROSE BUSHES FOR PLANTING

Ideally, bare-root roses should be planted as soon as received from the nursery or the mailman and as early in the new season as possible.

If after you receive them in the mail you cannot plant them right away because of soil or weather conditions, remove the packing, soak it in water, squeeze out surplus so it is damp but doesn't drip, then repack it around the roots. Store in a cool, dark place such as a garage or basement. See that the packing does not dry out when stored; renew moisture as needed.

A better method is to heel in bushes while waiting for an appropriate time to plant. Dig a shallow trench in a shaded place, lay the plants at a slant, cover the roots with soil, and wet the soil thoroughly. Do not leave them heeled in for too long a period. They should be planted when the buds break out.

Examine Rose Bush Before Planting

It pays to examine your new rose plants with care before you set them into the ground.

The plants should measure up to the standard of plant purchased. They should not be weak or spindly; the root system should not be badly cut up in harvesting or broken in shipping. (There will nearly always be a slight breakage in packing and shipping, but it should not be excessive in respect to the main roots.)

Plants shipped during severe winter weather are sometimes frozen in transit. Freezing breaks up the structure of the canes and usually turns the roots black. Even if they are carefully thawed, they are practically worthless.

Very rarely will you receive a diseased or dead plant. Symptoms of disease are almost impossible for anyone but a rose expert to detect in bare-root planting stock. If you have reason to suspect your purchase of being diseased, take it to your nurseryman, your County Agent, or an experienced rosarian.

If there is a correct reason for returning a defective rose, you are well protected by your nurseryman's guarantee. Be fair with your nurseryman in the matter of replacing stock and he will be fair with you.

How to Revive Dried-up Plants

Nurseries that sell plants by mail take great care to prepare rose bushes for shipping so they will arrive plump and fresh. Occasionally, however, plants will be delayed en route or will be subjected to dry heat during the shipping period and the packing may become dried out.

It is thus possible to receive plants in dried-up condition, even from the most reputable firms. The bark of the canes may have a shriveled appearance; and the bushes may be noticeably light in weight, due to the loss of normal moisture, and will lack the juicy green texture and quality of fresh stock. Bushes in this condition will be abnormally slow in starting growth—if they start at all.

Usually, dried-out rose plants can be restored to their naturally succulent state by very simple treatment. Here are two methods:

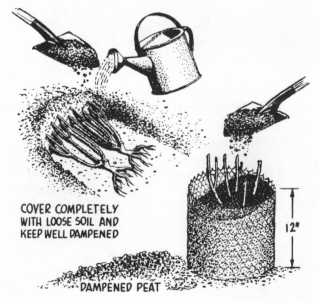

COVER COMPLETELY WITH LOOSE SOIL AND KEEP WELL DAMPENED

12"

DAMPENED PEAT

1. Lay the plants in a shallow trench and cover both roots and tops with wet earth. Keep the soil moist for about a week. Remove the plants carefully to avoid injuring any shoots that may have started. Usually, this treatment will refresh the bushes sufficiently to restore them to good planting condition.

If your plants are so dried out that they do not respond to this treatment, you may return them to their source accompanied by a letter reporting the condition of receipt. Most nurseries will gladly replace the plants.

2. Often, a dried-out bush can be restored by planting it and packing damp peat moss around the aboveground parts. Many a bush has been saved by this process that would otherwise have been lost.

Plant the bush in the manner described a little later in this chapter. Then, encircle the plant with a miniature fence of 1-inch mesh chicken wire, 12 inches tall. Cut a strip 36 inches long, form it into a cylinder, and wire the ends together. Place this around the rose bush and fill in with previously well dampened peat moss. Press the damp peat firmly against all parts of the bush. Dampen the peat around the plant for about two weeks, then inspect the plant for green shoots. If they have started, remove the wire cage and the peat. Be careful not to injure the tender new shoots when you take away the covering.

Incidentally, this same procedure can sometimes be used to revive a previously planted bush that has been allowed to dry out from lack of water or from drying wind action.

PREPARING SOIL FOR PLANTING

If you are fortunate enough to have a garden with fair-to-good loam topping the first 14 to 16 inches, you can probably get by without any soil improvement. But if you would like to give your roses the best opportunity to develop, you will want to mix up a quantity of a planting mixture to be filled into the planting holes.

A well tried, basic formula for a planting mix can be made up as follows:

7 parts loam, preferably on sandy side
2 parts leaf mold
1 part alfalfa meal
1 6-inch potful of bone meal to each barrowload of the blend.

If your loam is too heavy, mix in 1 or 2 parts of coarse sand. Alfalfa meal is a comparatively new but valuable component of soils for rose growing. It contributes a goodly portion of slowly assimilated nitrogen, improves soil structure, and increases its permeability.

If you cannot obtain either leaf mold or alfalfa meal, substitute for the leaf mold 1½ parts of peat moss; and for the alfalfa meal, 1½ parts well rotted manure, preferably steer or cow manure.

Manures other than cow or steer are not always acceptable. However, you can add them to the compost pile and use them later as an ingredient of compost.

Whatever formula you use—and you will run across others in your neighbors' gardens and in other books—mix it well. If possible, mix it two or three months before planting time. Turn it over from time to time and dampen it slightly every once in a while. This will serve to mellow and tone up the mixture.

Rebuilding Poor Soil

If your garden soil is of doubtful or poor quality, you may want to rebuild the entire top 16 inches in the rose bed. Such treatment may seem like an heroic undertaking if the bed is a large one; but it will prove to be a sound investment of material, time, and labor, because it will yield permanent soil improvement.

To renew the soil in a planting bed, start work three to five months ahead of your anticipated time for planting. Here's what to do:

1. Spread 2 or 4 inches of manure or rich compost over the area.

2. Sprinkle bone meal on top of this covering, at the rate of 8 to 10 pounds per 100 square feet.

3. Spade these materials into the soil, mixing them in thoroughly to a depth of about 14 inches.

4. Wet down the area and re-spade at least once a month up to planting time—if soil and weather conditions permit.

5. When the time for planting your bushes arrives, mix a quantity of planting soil, following the formula set forth above. Use this mixture to fill in the holes when you plant the rose bushes.

Of course there is still another alternative and one that is to be favored if your garden budget permits—order a load of rich garden loam to cover your bed to a depth of about 16 inches, and enclose the bed with a low retaining wall. Loam is sold by the cubic yard or by the ton, depending on local custom. One cubic yard will cover about 20 square feet of bed to a depth of 16 inches; a ton will cover about 15 square feet. Buy your loam only from a reputable dealer.

Soil Alkalinity

Roses prefer a slightly acid soil, around pH 6.0 to 6.5. If you suspect your soil of being too alkaline for rose culture, send a sample of it to a professional testing service for analysis. Your nursery, County Agent, or grower can usually tell you where to ship it. Be sure to mix up a *representative* sample, made of a blend of samples taken from 4 or 5 different points within the suspected area. Samples must be taken from the root area, at least 6 inches below the surface. Samples skimmed from the surface alone are completely unreliable.

Best and safest material for correcting over-alkalinity is common agricultural sulfur (not dusting sulfur). This should be applied to the soil in early spring at the rate of 2 pounds per 100 square feet.

PLANTING BARE-ROOT ROSES

Your rose plants have passed your critical inspection, they are awaiting their turn in the garden, and you are now ready to plant them. Here are the 12 simple steps to take:

1. Place bushes with their roots in a bucket of water or cover them with wet sacks. Do not let them be exposed to sunshine or drying wind. Some prefer to let the plants soak for 24 hours before setting out, but if yours seem plump and succulent, you need not follow this practice.

2. Dig a hole 16 inches deep and 18 to 20 inches wide, depending on the spread of the roots to be fitted into the hole.

If you are planting several roses, dig a trench or excavate individual holes. If you are planting several roses in a straight row, trenching is easier and works out for better planting.

For hybrid tea bush roses, space the holes not less than 24 inches from the center of the plant (bud union) to the center of the nearest plant. (See notes on spacing in chapter on planning a garden.)

Space tree roses not less than 4 feet apart. This spacing distance is usually determined by the decorative uses and placing of the tree in your garden arrangement.

For climbers, dig holes the same diameter and depth, with their edge right up to the object that the roses will climb; and space holes no closer than 6 feet apart from center of plant to center of nearest plant. Vigorous climbers should preferably be spaced about 10 feet apart.

When planting a tree rose, locate the stake in its proper place at the time of planting. Before pounding down the stake, place the tree temporarily in the hole you have dug and mark where the stake should go. It should be placed unobtrusively on the side away from where the tree will be most generally viewed.

The stake should not interfere with the large roots of the plant.

If you are planting rows of tree roses, for good appearance use stakes of uniform size, height, and color, and locate them all on the same side of the standards.

3. Fill the hole or trench about half full of garden soil, or the prepared mix described in an earlier section. Press the soil down firmly to prevent the formation of air pockets, but don't pack it solid because it will then become a hard mass that the roots will be unable to penetrate.

4. Now form a cone-shaped mound of earth in the center of the hole. Firm it down to prevent air pockets, as above. The top of the cone should be about 3 inches below ground level. To check this, lay a straight stick across the top of the hole.

5. Withdraw one plant at a time from your bucket and prepare it for planting. Cut off all bruised or broken roots with a sharp knife or keen pruning shears. The knife is preferred over the shears as it is more likely to give a clean-cut edge and less liable to cause dieback. Make cuts with a downward slanting angle about an inch above each break or bruise. Trim off the tip of each remaining root an inch or so to encourage quick formation of new feeding roots. Root cuts must not be painted with pruning dressing.

NOTE: If the plant has a generous root system, enlarge the hole to accommodate it instead of cutting the roots to fit the hole. The roots contain much of the food needed to start the plant on its spring push, and they should be shortened as little as possible.

6. Place the bush on the cone of soil so the crown rests on the top and the roots spread naturally down its slope. Fill in with soil until the roots are covered, packing it gently but firmly in place.

7. Fill the hole with water, let it drain out, and fill again. After the water has settled the second time, fill up the hole with soil. Let the soil come above ground level to allow for settling. Do not water again.

At this point, the bud union (a knot-like formation on the stem above the roots) should be about 2 inches above ground level. Tree roses can be planted with the bud union level or slightly below the surface. Check it by laying a straight stick across the hole at ground level.

If the bush has settled lower than 2 inches by the following morning, pull it up gently with a pumping motion to the proper height.

8. Form a protective mound of dirt around the plant to a height of 6 to 8 inches above the bud union. This will prevent the bush from drying out before it starts to grow. Wind action is particularly drying to new plantings. Keep this mound damp and in place.

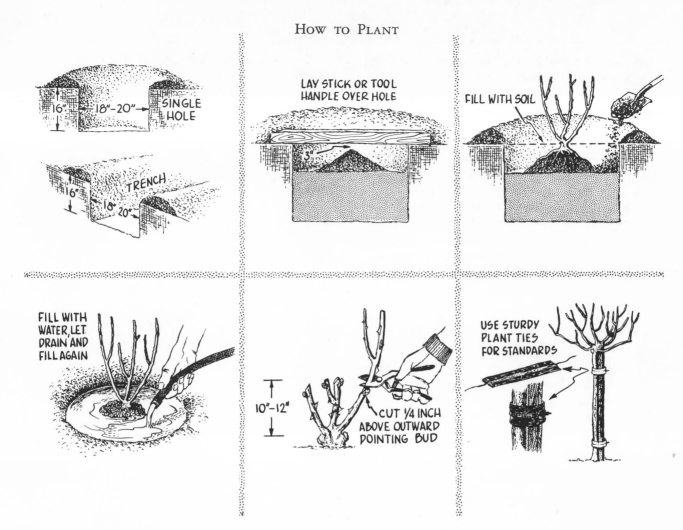

Key pointers in planting bush and standard roses

When growth is well started, remove the shielding soil to ground level.

9. When planting roses in isolated positions or some distance apart, many growers form a basin about the plant with a 3-foot ring of soil 3 to 4 inches high. This is useful in watering (see section on watering) and provides a convenient container for mulches. It must be noted that if appearance of the beds in your rose garden is a factor, you may not consider these basins desirable.

10. When planting is completed, cut back the canes to a length of 10 to 12 inches, if they were not previously trimmed to this length by the dealer. Cut as in pruning, with a slanting cut ¼ inch above an outward-pointing bud. *Exception:* Do not trim canes of tree roses, climbers, or ramblers. See next point.

11. Attach the central stem of the tree roses to the supporting stake with a slightly loose loop of strong cord or, better, with one of several loop devices made for this purpose and sold at nurseries. Climbers and ramblers should be securely but loosely fastened to the arbor or fence that they will be growing upon. Do not cut back the canes of climbers or ramblers.

12. Loosen the wires of any identifying name tags that may be attached to the branches. These tags should hang loose. If wrapped tightly around a cane or branch, the wire will girdle and possibly kill the rose.

The matter of a permanent label is a vexing one. Very few that are used are lasting. Permanent name plates to be poked into the soil at the base of the plants are used in some gardens, but they are expensive in quantity and they are easily dislodged by the gardener.

The common wood tags with copper wire hangers will last two or three years if the name lettering is done with black wax marking pencil.

Aluminum name tags are cheap and durable if they are hung loosely onto the bush with a piece of copper wire inserted in a hole punched in the body of the tag. The tiny strips of aluminum furnished with the tags for tying corrode and break off soon after using.

Cold-Weather Region Procedure

The procedure set forth above is standard for mild-weather areas. For localities that experience severe winter cold and freezing soil, the routine differs slightly, mainly in the depth of planting. In cold regions, it is desirable to set the bud union below ground level, preferably about 2 inches after the soil has settled.

To establish the plant at this level, you will need to dig the hole a little deeper and form a cone to within 5 inches of ground level.

POST-PLANTING CARE

Now that your plants are set out, you have little more to do. If the plants are good and you planted them properly, they will get along.

The most important aid that you can give them is to make sure that they do not dry out during the growing period. Keep them well watered, following the simple principles set forth in the chapter on watering.

One critical caution should be mentioned: Do not place fertilizer of any type around or below the roots or on top of the ground at planting time. All the nutrition necessary for the newly planted rose is in the planting mixture if it was properly prepared. Any excess of fertilizer around the new bush can retard or even prevent root growth. Many roses are ruined by being over-fed before their feeding roots are ready to assimilate the nutrition.

Keep an eye on your plants as they grow, but if you have set out many bushes, don't be alarmed if one or two of them lag behind the others in development.

Rose plants often develop at different rates. Some root stocks that they are budded on push out the buds sooner than others. The bushes may have been harvested at different times or stored under different conditions. Give them all plenty of time and abundant water. Once they have become established, the laggards will probably catch up with the faster ones before mid-season.

Mounding up with a mixture of half wet peat and half soil will often speed development.

PLANTING ROSES FROM CONTAINERS

There are only a few tricks to planting roses from cans, pots, or tar-paper containers. They may be planted anytime during the year.

Dig a hole about 6 inches larger all around than the container. Cut down the container on opposite sides if the nurseryman didn't do it for you. Remove the plant from the slit container and slide it into the hole.

In cold climates, set plant about 4 inches deeper than the bud union.

Some growers favor cutting off the bottom of the can, placing can and all in the hole, and then slitting the side of the can and removing it. This minimizes root injury and makes it easier to lower the root ball into the hole without its disintegrating as you handle it.

Set hybrid tea plants from 24 to 30 inches apart between centers of plants; floribundas 18 to 24 inches apart. Water them often enough to keep the soil moist. Be prepared to shade them if the weather turns hot or if they show signs of wilting.

If space is ample, form a watering basin around the planting site. It should cover an area about equal to the expected, ultimate spread of the bush.

In especially windy locations or areas, drive in stakes near the plant to steady it until the roots can securely anchor the bush in the ground.

Spread a 2 to 3-inch mulch over the bed to make the need for watering less frequent, to insure cool, moist earth for the roots, and to keep down weeds. Keep mulch at least 6 inches away from the bud union. Small plants that serve the same purpose as a mulch are thyme, mossy saxifrage, and viola. These and other low plants also add color and pattern to the rose garden. Their roots do not compete with the rose roots for food. (However, remember to protect these plants when you spray your roses. Some sprays used on roses are too strong for these ground covers.)

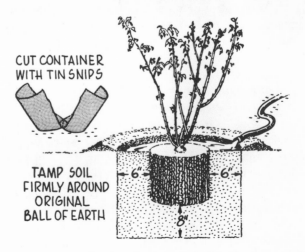

CUT CONTAINER WITH TIN SNIPS

TAMP SOIL FIRMLY AROUND ORIGINAL BALL OF EARTH

6"   6"

8"

Planting from a container

CHAPTER SIX

How to Water Your Roses

The rose is a thirsty plant. Rose bushes will usually survive if they are skimpily supplied with water, but they perform at their vigorous best only when their roots are kept well watered during the growing season.

In many areas in the West, where no rain falls for four or five months, few rose gardens receive even half of the water that they should for satisfactory growth and flower production. Even in regions where the rainfall is considered ample, occasional irrigation benefits rose plants.

HOW MUCH WATER DO ROSES NEED?

The exact amount that any one rose bush may require cannot be stated, because of the variations in climate and soil conditions. A few general rules will guide you to proper watering.

1. Rose roots should be kept damp but the soil about them should never be in a state of saturation for a prolonged period. Such saturation, "standing water," prevents oxygen from being absorbed by the roots and would probably cause the soil to turn sour and the plant to sicken. Roses must have good drainage to prevent overwatering which can cause severe injury to the plant. Drainage should be definitely assured at planting time.

The prime objective is to see that your roses get enough water, enough for vigorous growth at all times of the year.

2. Watering to the full root depth produces the best results. This means penetration of at least 16 to 18 inches. A moisture coverage to a depth of 12 inches is beneficial, but not so rewarding as deeper watering.

3. How can you tell if the water has penetrated to the desired depth? There are two ways: one is to dig down and find out for yourself; the other is to time the application of water to match the known ability of the soil to absorb it.

For one thing, if a casual probing of the surface reveals that the first 2 inches of the soil are dry, you can accept that as a signal to start watering. Second test is to dig down 16 to 18 inches the day after watering and find out how far down the water penetrated. To give meaning to your digging, you should know just how long you ran the hose the day before. You thus know that if an hour's irrigation only penetrated 10 inches, you will need to double the time next watering.

To gauge your water according to soil type, here are some handy rules of thumb based on studies made by the University of California:

1 cubic inch of water on top of the ground will wet directly downward:

   12 inches in sandy soil
   6 to 10 inches in loam
   4 to 5 inches in clay

To wet the soil down 2 feet in an area 2 x 2 feet (about the area of a rose basin) will require:

   5 gallons of water in sandy soil
   7.6 gallons in loam
   13.2 gallons in clay

These figures will show the relative volume of water required to irrigate different common types of soil.

HOW OFTEN SHOULD YOU WATER?

Roses need water all year. In most areas, rain or snow supplies sufficient root moisture for the plants during their dormant season; but in some arid sections of the West, occasional watering is needed even during winter months because the plants are not completely dormant and throughout the winter there are periods of little rain and drying winds.

The period when roses need plentiful irrigation, however, is from spring through early summer, when the bushes are enjoying their most active growth. In most areas, irrigation is needed at this time, either to supplement spring and early summer rains or to supply the plants' entire needs. In many parts of the West, the rose is at the mercy of the garden hose and would not live for very long if denied regular and generous irrigation.

If your watering plans are dictated by your spring-summer climate, you are also regulated by the type of soil in your rose bed. As mentioned above, soils absorb water in differing quantities, according to their texture. Water is quickly absorbed by sandy soils—and also quickly exhausted. Clay soils take in the water slowly,

but they give it up slowly, too. Thus, if your garden soil is sandy in texture, you can expect to water more frequently than you would if it were clay. You will also have to apply more water, because of the relatively large amount that is lost by evaporation or other causes.

Here are the rules of thumb that you can follow:

Soil type	Watering interval
Sandy	4 to 10 days
Loam	8 to 15 days
Clay	15 to 30 days

During hot, dry spells, it will be necessary to water more frequently. A day of hot, dry wind will draw out

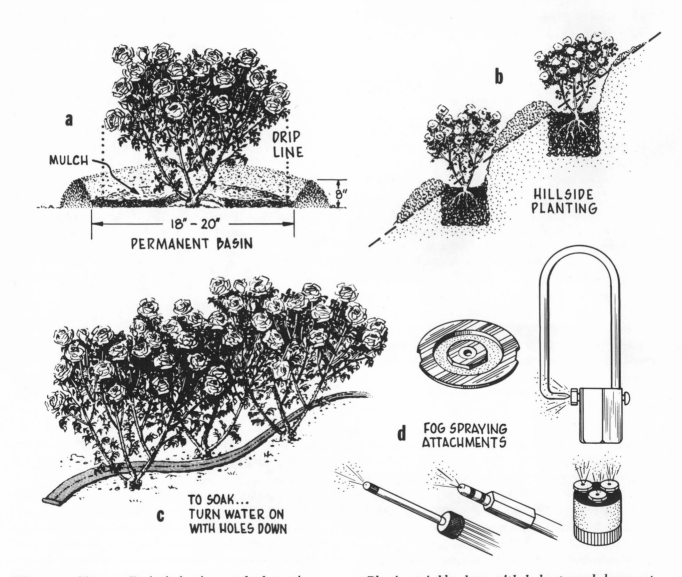

WATERING TIPS: *a. Basin irrigation method, particularly good in arid climate. b. To make hillside basins, form mound on downhill side using excavated soil.*

c. Plastic sprinkler hose with holes turned down gets water under mulch. d. Fog spray nozzles provide gentle spray, use with caution to avoid black spot

52

of the leaves a great deal of water which will require prompt replacement in the root zone.

With roses, as with other garden plants, you should keep in mind the golden rule of watering: *Water deeply —but only as often as necessary.* It is better to let the soil dry out slightly and to allow the plant to draw heavily on its reservoir of water before filling it up again than to water too frequently. If water is applied too often, it encourages shallow rooting. The frequently and lightly applied water does not penetrate very far below the surface; and the feeding roots stay within the shallow, damp zone where they are subject to injury from cultivating or weeding, may be burned by fertilizer concentrations, or may be damaged by a drying out of the top soil.

METHODS OF WATERING

Roses may be amply supplied with water by flood irrigation or by overhead watering.

The best and simplest method is by flood irrigation. This may be by direct application of the hose stream inside of simple earthen wall basins around one or more bushes or entire beds, or by a perforated, plastic sprinkling hose turned over with its holes facing downward.

Basin Irrigation

Although some growers object to the appearance of basins —considering them aesthetically unsatisfactory—nevertheless, basin irrigation is an efficient way of applying water in quantities to one or a dozen rose bushes at the same time. In some areas in the Southwest, basin irrigation is an absolute necessity because of the arid climate.

Make permanent basins at planting time around each plant or around the entire bed. In hot sections, this means a well tamped ridge 8 inches high; in cooler areas it can be lower. Once made, it should be there to stay to concentrate water around the roots where it is needed. The ridge, too, holds mulches, manure, and fertilizer in place.

With established plants, don't try to make ridges by hoeing soil around them. Any disturbance of the surface near the plant can seriously damage its feeder roots, some of which are almost on top of the ground. Instead, haul soil from another part of the garden. If your soil is sandy in texture, work in a little clay or adobe to stiffen the ridge.

Basins around single bushes should be 18 to 20 inches in diameter. The rim of the basin should encircle the bush just beyond the drip line, or the anticipated drip line of a newly planted bush. Growing roses on a slop-ing hillside presents real watering problems. About the only way one can irrigate hillside roses thoroughly and without excessive run-off waste of water is by the use of basins around one or more bushes.

For guidance in making a hillside basin, see the drawings.

Applying Water

One of the best means of applying water at ground level is to use a plastic sprinkler hose, the kind that shoots out a fine mist from hundreds of tiny holes spaced along its entire length. One of these can be twisted through the rose garden to irrigate almost any layout of rose bushes. Because the water is given off in a fine mist, it soaks into the soil and does not run off. The device should be turned on lightly. Some sprinkler hoses are made with two attached parallel tubes. These lay flat and can be used with the spray going upward or with the holes underneath. In the latter position they do a superb job of irrigating wherever desired without continually wetting the foliage.

Direct hose watering hardly requires instructions. Any method can be employed that gets an ample supply of water into the soil about the roots. The stream can be directed and better applied by one of the "water wand" devices which breaks the nozzle force of the stream and prevents scouring of the soil. The long handle of the wand enables one to direct the stream to any desired point. Other simple devices to prevent soil erosion are small earthen flower pots or jars placed over the nozzle or rags or old socks tied around it.

Irrigating Mulched Beds

When irrigating a rose bed on which you have placed a thick mulch of peat, manures and some other materials, it is usually difficult to get the water flowing freely through all parts of the sun-dried mulch, particularly when the mulch covers the entire area around the roses.

It is well to have a space around each rose bush clear of the mulch down to the soil surface for about 6 inches on each side of the rose stem. This forms a basin for the entrance of irrigation water directly to the roots.

When irrigating with a double-tube plastic sprinkling hose, lay holes down in a temporary narrow depression or ditch quickly scratched in the mulch at the edge of the bed or zigzagged through the plantings. This directs the flow of the water under the mulch directly into the soil and also saturates the mulch from the ground side upward. This takes only minutes to do and does make for more thorough irrigation. When running water on the upper surface of the mulch, some dry areas resist its penetration. Irrigation water must penetrate to the soil surface beneath the mulch.

Overhead Sprinklers

In hot, dry climates, overhead sprinkling works very well, helping to keep humidity high and foliage fresh.

The sprinklers should be turned on during the day, so the plants can dry off before nightfall and thus resist mildew attack. Best time is early in the morning, when the temperature is on the rise.

Do not wet foliage in brilliant sunlight. To do so will risk burning the leaves and blossoms.

Mist-type sprinkler heads are considered best. The sprinkler hose mentioned above can also be used for this type of irrigation by turning the pressure high.

Remember that overhead sprinkling washes insecticidal dusts and spray residues from the foliage. You will therefore need to treat your roses frequently during the months of heaviest irrigation. The best time to apply a dust is right after you have watered, while the leaves are still damp. Insecticides, on the other hand, should be applied when the leaves are dry; otherwise the excess moisture on the foliage will dilute the formula.

Objections to Overhead Sprinklers

Overhead sprinkling does have serious drawbacks in any area where black spot or rose leaf rust are prevalent.

Even in areas where black spot is rarely noted, the use of overhead sprinkling will encourage the incidence of this serious rose disease and spread its spores over the entire rose-growing area. It will also increase the spread of mildew.

One should not install overhead sprinklers in a rose garden until the above factors of disease encouragement have been studied with local rosarians who have had experience with them.

If you plan to install a permanent sprinkler system, lay it out so the sprinkler heads overlap each other one-half in coverage. This will insure uniform water penetration throughout the rose bed.

Foliage Rinsing

Whether you irrigate by flooding or by overhead watering, you can contribute to the appearance and health of your rose plants by hosing off the foliage every week or so. The best time to do this is the day before you spray or dust. A brisk rinsing keeps the leaves from becoming choked with dust, and, incidentally, may knock off a few aphis and spider-mites.

WAYS TO CONSERVE WATER

In localities that experience long stretches of arid weather or that encounter an annual water shortage, the rose grower can use several proven methods of conserving water.

1. A good mulch will save many gallons of water and will keep the root area cool and moist. Your choice is wide open, but influenced by availability in your area. Mulches are discussed in the next chapter, but here is a recap for your guidance: lawn clippings, straw, ground corn husks, sawdust, steer or cow manure, peat moss, etc. Better than straight peat moss is a mix of $\frac{1}{2}$ peat moss, $\frac{1}{2}$ cow or steer manure, or $\frac{1}{2}$ peat moss and $\frac{1}{2}$ ground corn husks or sawdust. Straight peat moss becomes rather impervious to water after several waterings and dryings in the sun.

When you probe under the mulch to determine how damp the soil is, don't be misled by surface moisture in the early morning. This is most likely dew condensed from the mulch. The soil under it may be bone dry once you get below the damp surface.

2. Another way of saving water is to be systematic about your watering practices. Find out just how much water your roses need, just how long to run the hose, and don't give your roses much more than they need. If you are gadget-minded, you can purchase timing devices that remember for you and shut off the water after a predetermined interval. A written record or even a marked-up calendar in the garage can turn out to be well worth the small amount of time it exacts. They will help you keep to a regular schedule.

3. If the surface of the ground has not been mulched, a light scratching of the soil the day after watering will prevent its caking. This practice was once thought to draw subsoil moisture to the surface, but this is now known to be untrue. The advantage of preventing the soil from caking is that it will admit more air to the roots and will also allow the soil to accept water and fertilizing nutrients more quickly the next time you irrigate.

CHAPTER SEVEN

How to Feed Your Roses

For all practical purposes there are three ways in which to feed your roses:

1. By application of fertilizing materials to the soil surface above the roots.

2. By leaf feeding, that is, spraying the foliage with highly nitrogenous materials.

3. By a mulch of manure, leaf mold, enriched peat moss, or other organic substances.

FERTILIZING

Like most plants, roses require three major food elements for healthy growth: nitrogen, phosphorus (phosphoric acid), and potassium. These basic elements are present in varied quantities in all garden soils; however, plants diminish the supply and sooner or later the elements must be replenished.

Nitrogen is the element that produces the green growth of plants, and, combined with other elements, it is an important constituent of chlorophyll.

During the main period of growth, a large amount of the nitrogen required by the plant comes from the decomposition of organic materials in the soil, but the major portion must be supplied by the gardener.

No other element so rapidly improves plant growth. Properly applied, its effects are quickly shown in increased growth, more intense green color, and greater size of leaves. Its beneficial effects are further revealed in the quantity and quality of the blooms.

Phosphorus (phosphoric acid) provides the most help during the period when the plant blooms. The supply of phosphorus in soils is easily made unavailable by chemical "lock"; it becomes unavailable because of excessive acidity or alkalinity of the soil. In many soils, phosphorus will not leach or wash down into the soil after surface application. This is the one reason for incorporating phosphorus in the soil at planting time.

Potash (potassium) assists both nitrogen and phosphorus in the performance of their particular functions.

TYPES OF FERTILIZERS

You can use either organic or inorganic fertilizers in your rose garden. Both are effective and each has its respective advantages.

Inorganics are quicker acting than organics and they contain the basic elements in more concentrated form. It would require a ton of manure to supply the amount of nitrogen available from a 25-pound bag of ammonium sulfate. On the other hand, the inorganics do not contribute humus to the soil.

A well rounded program of rose feeding employs both types.

INORGANIC FERTILIZERS

Inorganic fertilizers are chemical compounds that release the three basic elements—nitrogen, phosphorus, and potassium—when mixed into the soil and watered. In their pure state, these elements are not usable—nitrogen is a gas, potassium is a metal, phosphorus is an unstable substance used in chemical warfare—but when united with other elements in compounds, they are harnessed for garden use. Thus, the fertilizer label that states that a given brand contains 4 per cent nitrogen indicates that the remaining 96 per cent of the bag's contents is made up of another substance needed to make the nitrogen usable in the soil, plus a filler which makes spreading easier.

The gardener can buy chemical fertilizers as separate elements for specific use, or he can buy the elements blended into a "complete fertilizer." If he buys the separate elements, he would purchase:

Nitrogen—ammonium sulfate, ammonium nitrate, sodium nitrate, or calcium nitrate. All of these are applied at the rate of 1 pound per 100 square feet, except ammonium nitrate which is applied in half this quantity. Another compound, ammonium phosphate combines nitrogen and phosphorus in one package.

Phosphorus—superphosphate, treble (concentrated) superphosphate, or ammonium phosphate, as stated above.

Potassium—potash. Wood ashes are a common source of potash.

Most gardeners prefer to use the complete commercial fertilizers that consist of a blend of the three basic elements, mixed in varying proportions to suit different soil and climatic conditions throughout the country.

By legal requirement, the formula for the mixture is printed on the label of each container. It is given in percentages, as:

Nitrogen.................................4.00%
Phosphoric acid.........................8.00%
Potash....................................4.00%

In referring to fertilizer blends, gardeners simply abbreviate the formulas to the figures that stand for the quantities of nitrogen, phosphorus, and potash in the mixture. The above, for instance, is a 4-8-4 fertilizer.

A formula of 4-12-4 is considered a well balanced blend, but formulations containing much higher percentages may also be obtained.

Pellet Fertilizers

A new and practical method of preparing commercial fertilizers is by pelletizing them.

The small, round, pea-sized pellets are much easier to apply than the same material in powder form. A handful can be tossed exactly where you want them, an obvious advantage to gardeners with a large number of roses— particularly when mass plantings or hard-to-get-at areas make the rose root areas well-nigh inaccessible. Another advantage of the pellets is that they dissolve slower than the powdered fertilizers, so that their nutrient action covers a longer period with greater efficiency.

A formula of 16-16-8 is very satisfactory, and will give vigorous growth with large leaves and flowers over an extended period of time; feeding three times a year should be sufficient if you are using pellets with this ratio.

When To Apply

Application of fertilizers should be synchronized with the blooming periods of your roses so the plants will receive the food when they need it, which is just before they break into bloom.

The cycle of growth from the start of the flowering shoot to the opening of the bud covers 5 to 6 weeks; so it is well to fertilize approximately 6 weeks before each blooming period.

In California, for example, roses usually bloom four times a year and thus require quarterly feeding. The first big crop of blooms, which arrives about May 1, calls for application of fertilizer about March 20. The second crop, which comes about June 20, calls for fertilization about May 10. The third crop of August 15 would be fertilized about July 1; the fourth, in October, should be fed about September 1.

In areas where fewer blossoming periods are the rule, fewer fertilizings would also be required. Also, in localities that experience heavy winter freeze or early frost, the last application should be light, to prevent the plant from bursting into new growth that would be killed by the onset of winter. The first spring feeding should be the heaviest, because of the demands of the spring flowering.

If you keep a written record of the blooming dates of your own rose bushes, you can easily establish your own feeding calendar.

How To Apply

To apply commercial fertilizers:

1. Wet down the soil the day before applying in order to avoid root burn.

2. Scratch the soil surface lightly, then sprinkle the fertilizer around the root areas keeping it at least 4 inches away from the main stems.

3. Apply at the rate of 3 pounds per 100 square feet of planting area, or 1 heaping tablespoon per plant.

4. Soak in the fertilizer thoroughly.

Newly Planted Roses

If soil is prepared as mentioned on page 47, newly-planted roses needn't be fertilized until after the first flush of bloom — there is enough nutrition in the planting soil for initial growth. Healthy new plants also have considerable stored food in roots and stems.

ORGANIC FERTILIZERS

Organic fertilizing materials are many and varied, most of them derived from animal products. Animal manures make up the bulk of this class of fertilizer. Other organics of value for rose feeding are: liquid fish fertilizers, bone meal, blood meal, cottonseed meal, and, of course, compost.

Organic fertilizers supply the same elements that the

inorganics do, but some of them have the additional value of helping to maintain the humus content of the soil and to supplement the soil bacteria population. Humus and accompanying soil bacteria aid in rendering available the various plant foods from the mineral compounds in the soil, and they also improve the physical condition of the soil.

Manures

The best animal fertilizers for feeding and mulching roses are the steer, cow, and sheep manures. Horse, pig, and chicken manures may also be used, preferably after having been converted, broken up, and mellowed well in your compost pile.

Steer manure is slightly better than cow manure, as its content generally has slightly more nitrogen. Steer manure typically contains approximately 1.5% nitrogen, cow manure half that amount, and sheep manure 2½% nitrogen. All are good soil builders.

Animal manures build up the soil and can improve its texture and aeration. They become converted into humus and, as such, provide a valuable source of plant food and nutrition for soil bacteria. In short, manures are practically a "must" for the best culture of roses.

If the manures are not applied as a mulch, they can, of course, be used as fertilizers. As such they should be spread around the root areas of the plants to a depth of 2 or 3 inches. On the Pacific Coast, apply them in February or March and again in June. In colder areas, apply them when the frost is out of the ground.

Supplement manure feeding with the recommended feedings of "commercial" or liquid fish fertilizers.

Liquid Fish Fertilizers

Liquid fertilizers are justifiably popular because of their simplicity of application and their ready absorption by the plant.

When used with a hose attachment, they can be applied quickly and thoroughly over a large rose garden. Their nutrient elements are almost immediately made available to the plant, and a quick response often results. Some formulations also aid in the maintenance of the humus content of garden soil.

Liquid fertilizers can be obtained in an extensive choice of brands and formulas, in either organic or inorganic mixtures. They may be procured in completely balanced specifications, such as 15-5-5. Some of these fertilizers can be used in leaf feeding (see below).

Liquid fish fertilizers are exceptionally beneficial to roses. Some of them are derived solely from fish products; others combine fish products with a strengthening build-up of organic nitrogen, water-soluble phosphoric acid, and potash. Both types seem to have the ability to produce vigorous growth of foliage and flowers. Rosarians who have used the balanced formula 15-5-5 report luxurious foliage and a fine yield of blooms.

Bone Meal

Bone meal is one of our most valuable fertilizers because it is slow acting and long lasting. It has a high proportion of phosphoric acid but is low in nitrogen.

Because bone meal decomposes slowly and will not burn roots, it can be mixed with the soil around root areas. It can also be applied freely to the top soil around the plants, a heaping tablespoon to each plant.

Blood Meal

Blood meal is high in organic nitrogen, containing 12 to 14 per cent. It will produce rapid, luxuriant growth, but it must be used carefully, because an excess can cause root burn and spindly growth. Maximum feeding: 1 level tablespoon sprinkled around each plant.

For a quick growth pickup, some gardeners prefer one of the ammonium phosphates. These are better balanced rations than blood meal. Ammonium phosphate contains from 11 to 16 per cent nitrogen and 20 to 48 per cent available phosphoric acid. It, too, must be used in conservative quantities, according to the maker's instructions.

Calcium (Lime)

There is generally plenty of calcium in most soils, and in forms that plants can assimilate. It is rarely necessary to apply lime to the soil as fertilizer. If soil tests prove it to be lacking in any soil, the safest way to correct the deficiency is by application of ground limestone, at the rate of 2 tablespoonfuls to a rose bush. This material favors the growth of bacteria and gives soils a better tilth.

Cottonseed Meal

Cottonseed meal is an excellent organic rose food where heavy growth is desired. It has a content of 7 per cent nitrogen, 3 per cent phosphoric acid and 2 per cent potash. Its reaction is on the acid side.

LEAF FEEDING

Application of nutrient materials through the leaves is not a new method of feeding roses, but it has recently become more widely practiced because of the introduction of products specifically designed for this purpose and because of the improvement in spraying devices for applying the solutions easily and effectively.

The method for feeding rose plants through their leaves is a simple one: the nutrient material is sprayed on the leaves like an insecticide. In fact, the concentrated food may be mixed with a fungicide or insecticide and the bush doctored and fed with one application.

When the nutrient solution is sprayed on the leaves, it is taken in through the stomata or breathing pores on the underside of the leaf and is almost immediately made available for the normal process of conversion into plant food.

Leaf feeding will not produce miracles, but carefully controlled experiments with various foliar feeding materials in several sections of the country have established several facts about the practice:

1. Leaf feeding is a valuable supplement to root feeding, but it doesn't replace it.

2. The practice usually increases the number of strong flower-producing canes branching from the lower parts of the plant.

3. It usually increases the production of flowers, often as much as 20 to 30 per cent, and the flowers are likely to be richer in color.

4. It will give the foliage a darker green color, will increase the size of the leaves and make them more disease-resistant.

5. Foliar feeding compounds are compatible with practically all insecticides and fungicides and can be applied in the same spray with them.

6. Leaf feeding is particularly effective in the early months of the year when the ground is cold and the roots do not readily take up the nitrogen in the soil.

How To Apply

For leaf feeding it is best to use one of the many good concentrated fertilizers especially recommended for the purpose. Many of the powdered commercial fertilizers can cause severe leaf burn. An organic fish fertilizer with a formula of 15-5-5, used at a strength of 2 teaspoons to the gallon of water, has given good results.

Here are rules for applying leaf-feeding solutions:

1. Be sure to spray the undersides of the leaves thoroughly. Material sprayed on the top sides is largely wasted.

2. When applying to shiny-leafed rose varieties, add a "spreader-sticker" to the solution to insure that the material will adhere to the slick leaf surface. Use 1/4 teaspoon of mild household detergent to a gallon of water.

3. Follow the directions on the label exactly. Quantities used in excess of those recommended can cause leaf burn.

4. Start the feeding program when the first leaves are formed in spring and continue feedings every 2 or 3 weeks until July 1.

MULCHING

Although a mulch is not primarily a method for feeding roses, it serves so many useful purposes, and contributes so much to the health and growth of your plants that it must be regarded as a prime factor in your rose gardening.

A mulch performs several functions:

1. It reduces evaporation of surface moisture and thereby conserves water.

2. It holds down the weed crop. If it is a heavy mulch, it usually prevents weed growth.

3. It eliminates need for cultivation by preventing surface crusting.

4. In warm weather, it tends to keep roots cool and moist.

5. If the mulch is made up of animal manures, it aids in the maintenance of the humus content and the bacteria of the soil and it feeds the roses.

What To Use

In areas where it is readily obtainable, well seasoned cow or steer manure makes the best mulch for rose beds. A 2 to 3-inch layer of this manure will do about everything that a good mulch should.

Other materials that are suitable: manure and peat moss in equal portions, well mixed; various leaf mold; bean straw; ground corn cob; and, of course, properly prepared composts. Sawdust is recommended if it is mixed with nitrogen fertilizers (6 lbs. ammonium sulfate per 100 lbs. sawdust) or half and half with manure.

Peat alone makes a poor rose mulch. It dries out quickly after the original wetting and, if allowed to dry out completely, becomes almost waterproof.

When applying any mulch, keep it 4 to 6 inches away from the main stalks. This leaves a small basin around the stem for ready entry of water, and prevents possible damage to the base of the rose.

When To Mulch

Apply the mulch in early spring in mild climates—around February first. In colder climates, apply it after the frost is well out of the ground—from 4 to 6 weeks before blooming time.

CHAPTER EIGHT

How to Prune and Train Roses

We prune to shape our rose bushes and improve their appearance, to encourage growth of new flowering wood and basal shoots, and to produce more and better flowers. Any one of these reasons justifies the operation.

Shaping a bush to achieve a symmetrical plant is perhaps the main object of pruning. A properly pruned rose should have a well balanced arrangement of canes, a center open to the light and air, and its flowering branches growing outward and upward.

When pruning, always keep this balanced symmetry in mind. A symmetrical, well pruned bush usually means a healthy, generous producer of blooms.

WHEN TO PRUNE

The time for pruning is everywhere determined by climatic conditions. Generally speaking, pruning should be done early in the spring, when the new growth started by the pruning will be reasonably safe from damage by frost.

The best time is toward the end of the dormant season, when the large, plump buds first begin to swell. Generally, that signal to prune comes to southern California in January; to central California from January 15 to February 1; to northern California (mountainous regions), western Oregon and Washington in late February through March; and to the country east of the high mountains in April.

However, in parts of western Oregon and Washington, where spring starts comparatively early but develops rather slowly, some rose experts recommend waiting to prune until 60 days before the approximate date on which you might expect the first blooms. For instance, if you look for the first roses in Redmond, Washington, on June 1, wait until April 1 to do your pruning.

All pruning dates for the western coastal states are subject to local conditions which vary greatly in distances as slight as fifty miles. Altitude and exposure to cold northern winds are important factors.

In the Gulf states, depending on the lateness of the seasons, pruning is usually done in January; in Alabama, in February; in the Great Lakes area, April 1 to May 1.

Do not delay your pruning into the growing season. This could result in a heavy bleeding of sap and a weakening of the plant's growth.

TOOLS FOR ROSE PRUNING

Provide yourself with a pair of sharp pruning shears and keep them sharp. A small keyhole saw is needed for removing the larger canes. A sharp knife with a strong blade, a can of grafting paint and, of course, a pair of stout leather gloves, complete the list of tools.

There are two types of pruning shears used for home rose gardening, and both have their advantages.

The older and more familiar type, doubtless the favorite of professional gardeners, is the drop-forged shears that have a curved, tool-steel cutting blade. When sharp and in good condition, this tool can make a clean, close cut. Best buys are imports from Europe.

The other type, known as the anvil shears, has a straight blade opposed by a flat bed of soft metal. They are lighter than the drop-forged shears and easier to keep sharp with a small oilstone. Women find them easier to use because they require less hand pressure.

Buy either type in a good quality, keep them clean and sharp, and they will serve you well.

BASIC PRUNING RULES

On the next page are nine basic rules for pruning roses. Later in this chapter, beginning on page 62, variations on these rules are discussed and illustrated under the different types of roses.

1. Remove all obviously dead wood.

2. Remove wood that is heavily scaled, sun-scalded, or covered with lesions.

3. Remove any branch that crosses through the center of the plant or that rubs heavily against any other branch.

4. Completely remove all suckers whenever they appear.

5. Remove branches that make the bush seem lopsided.

6. If some new, large basal canes formed during the preceding growing season, remove an old cane for each new one; this renews the plant.

7. Examine the wood that formed last year. Usually, you should cut it back to an outside bud eye. How much you cut back depends on the variety or the climate you live in, as discussed in detail later in this chapter.

8. Make all cuts on a 45-degree angle, $\frac{1}{4}$ inch above a strong leaf bud and running downward. Make the cuts with sharp pruning shears or a keen knife in order not to crush the cane or branch.

More bushes are ruined by the making of improper cuts than from any other cause. Cutting too far above the bud will invariably start dieback, which will sometimes destroy the entire cane.

9. Seal large cuts with asphalt pruning compound. Cover the cut ends of pencil-sized branches by poking a carpet tack into the tip. These precautions lessen drying out of cut ends and prevent borers from entering.

CUTTING FLOWERS AS A FORM OF PRUNING

Whenever you cut blooms from your rose bush, you are performing a pruning function. Cut off enough of the stem to provide support in the vase, but not so much that it deprives the growing plant of needed leaves. Recommended practice is to leave at least two sets of leaflets on the branch from which the flower has been cut. In cutting side branches, the best new growth comes from three or more buds away from the main cane.

When cutting back roses, where possible cut at a point where there is a "fat" bud starting in wood of the current year's growth or wood of one previous year, no older.

Cutting blooms with long stems from newly planted bushes is not recommended until the plants have become firmly established. Weak or ailing plants should not have their blooms cut with long stems. Merely snap off the spent bloom.

Withered or faded flowers should be snipped off throughout the growing season.

BUD RUBBING

"Bud rubbing" is a year-round supplement to pruning for control of unwanted growth.

As you work over your rose bushes, check the new growth buds starting on the canes.

Their position will indicate the location of the starting branches and the direction they will take in growth.

If the indication is that these branches will be poorly located or useless, that they will cross over the center or interfere with more desirable flowering canes, rub off the offending buds with your thumb.

By this elimination of useless growth, you conserve food and energy that would otherwise be wasted on unwanted branches and you prevent the growth of branches you would have to prune later if you permitted them to grow.

KNIFE PRUNING

Knife pruning is the method of experts. With a keen knife, you can secure cleaner, smoother cuts than with any shears. However, such pruning requires a strong, sure grip—and plenty of practice. In fact, it is prudent to try out the technique on bushes that you value lightly until you have mastered the knack. This is a case where practice makes perfect.

Although you can buy pruning knives, a good jack-knife with a top quality blade will serve you just as well. You should keep the knife edge keen by whetting it occasionally with a small oilstone.

To make the pruning cut:

1. Hold the cane you wish to eliminate in your gloved left hand.

2. Gripping the knife handle in the palm of your right hand, draw the blade through the cane with a quick movement. Cut upward and toward you, never away from you. The slanting cut should come $\frac{1}{4}$ inch above the bud eye, not level with it or below it.

3. To keep the roots from loosening as a result of the upward pull of your primary cuts, place one foot on the ground directly over the close-in root area when you make your cuts.

HIGH VS. LOW PRUNING

For many years, no detail of rose culture aroused more discussion and argument than the question of how far to cut back the canes at pruning time.

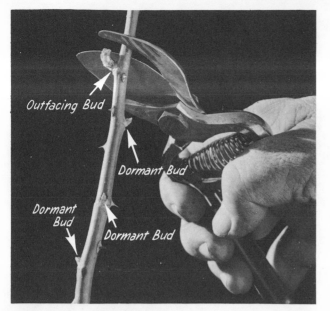

Rose cane being headed back to an outfacing bud. Next two dormant buds below it will probably grow shoots, too. Some dormant buds are only very small red dots

Suckers should always come out when you see them. You can always recognize a sucker by its point of origin below the bud union. Pare out base of sucker with knife

Rosarians divided themselves into two camps: One side favored cutting the bushes back drastically, leaving merely 2 or 3 bud eyes on each cane; the other group took a conservative position, favoring a light cutting back of the bushes in spring.

The argument still rages, but the consensus now seems to favor conservative pruning. As the American Rose Society puts it, "The modern practice is not to remove any more of the strong healthy wood than is necessary. Experiments have shown conclusively that the more wood you can retain, the larger the plants will be and the more blooms produced. The flower quality will also improve in size, color and stem length. Unwarranted severe pruning robs the plant of stored food and is one of the chief factors causing short-lived plants. A developing shoot is dependent upon the food stored in the cane to sustain growth until it is approximately 12 inches long." (*What Every Rose Grower Should Know,* 1951 ed.)

Of course, low pruning is sometimes unavoidable. In areas where low winter temperatures and killing frosts damage the canes, it is often necessary to cut back severely in spring to remove the damaged portions. Sometimes, too, a late frost following an unusually warm early spring, may catch a rose bush in bloom and freeze it to the ground. In such cases, deep cutting preserves the life of the plant, and the bush will respond swiftly to the treatment.

Sometimes, too, low pruning is advocated for producing exhibition-quality blossoms. The bush is cut

back sharply and the entire activity of the root system is channeled into the production of a few spectacular blooms. This method will produce prize-winning roses, it is true, but it is hard on the plant and it doesn't produce the garden display that most homeowners desire. Proper feeding and watering will produce large blooms on conservatively pruned bushes.

MANAGEMENT OF BASAL GROWTH AND SUCKERS

The first lesson in rose pruning is to learn to distinguish between the valuable new shoots growing up from the base or bud union of the plant, and the so-called "sucker growth" coming from below the bud union.

Sucker Growth

Suckers invariably grow from the wild understock roots. They can be clearly distinguished from the hybrid tea growth by the different appearance of their stems, foliage and thorns, and by the fact that they come from below the bud union. This point of origin alone can settle all doubt.

Sucker growth has a different, smaller leaf than the hybrid tea rose it accompanies. It has a slenderer stalk, smaller, softer thorns, and is a lighter green in color.

Whether or not a basal growth has leaves with 5 or 7 leaflets is no indication of its being a sucker. You can find groups of both 5 and 7 leaflets on many hybrid tea bushes and on most climbers and ramblers.

Sucker growth should be removed entirely whenever observed and identified. The longer it remains before removal, the more difficult the task becomes.

To remove suckers, work down below the bud union with your fingers or a small trowel to the point where the sucker growth starts from the wild root. At this point the sucker can usually be pulled or broken off the root. If the sucker is a large one and the wood has become hardened, remove part of the root wood along with the sucker.

If a sucker is cut or broken off at a point above where it originates and there are dormant eyes on the part remaining, one or more suckers will start to grow to bother you again.

Basal Growth

One often hears the comment that a certain rose "has reverted" to its wild origin. This can never happen. What might have occurred is that the sucker growth was permitted to grow freely, and even to "take over" and dominate the hybrid tea plant. This can lead to the partial or complete extinction of the hybrid tea.

Basal shoots constitute the natural annual renewal of the normal cane growth. This new wood must be retained. As stated before, the best and most flowers will later come on these new canes. These are the canes which grow up from the bud union or a point close above it. One or more are produced annually by a vigorous, healthy bush, and they are a vital factor in the continued renewal of the productive wood of the bush.

Too often, these valuable basal shoots are mistaken for sucker growth coming from below the bud union and are removed, injuring the plant. Be sure to identify properly any shoots growing from the base area before removing.

There are two ways of handling basal growth. Experience should tell you how best to handle it on your own plants.

1. Pinch off the tip of the new basal growth when it reaches a height of 12 or 14 inches. Permit the lateral (side branches) to develop to their full height and bloom. After blooming, cut them back to the third or fourth eye above their starting point.

2. Allow the basal shoot to grow fully and bloom. After blooming, cut back the center growth and each side branch to the first well developed bud.

Very often the basal shoot will develop into what is known as a "candelabra" growth. The top of the shoot branches, and each of the new branches will bear a relatively small bud and flower. After this branched top has bloomed out, remove it with a clean cut across the lowest crotch. (See illustration.) There will rarely be any dieback from the cuts above the crotch, and the first well developed bud below the crotch usually will produce a good lateral branch.

The cane will then develop normally without further candelabra growth.

AFTER-PRUNING PRACTICE

As a final step after pruning, it is a wise precaution to seal all cuts with an asphalt grafting paint. This applies chiefly to cuts on canes and branches larger than pencil size.

This sealing of pruning cuts prevents drying of the bark and dieback of canes, and discourages the entrance of borers into the centers of the canes.

After pruning is finished, a complete and thorough clean-up of the rose garden and its plants is a necessary procedure.

1. Remove all leaves remaining on your cut-back bushes, trees, and climbers, particularly the climbers. Be thorough; remove every leaf. It is these leaves of the past season's growth that harbor and carry over insect pests and spores of fungus diseases into the new season.

2. Rake up old leaves, trash, and cuttings from the ground areas of your rose beds and burn them.

Dead leaves usually accumulate and pack in around the bud union of your bushes. Dead leaves and trash are great breeders of fungus disease and insect pests.

3. Promptly after the garden cleanup, spray your cut-back bushes and the ground about them with 26 per cent calcium polysulfide. Use at the dosage recommended on the label. This is your last chance to apply dormant spray to kill the spores of mildew, rust and black spot on the plants, scale on the older canes, and insect pests wintering about the plants. Lime sulfur also is a secondary soil corrective for heavy soils.

PRUNING HYBRID TEA ROSES

What is a conservative pruning of hybrid tea bush roses? In areas of mild climatic conditions, free of killing frosts, it means cutting back your bushes to approximately one-half of the previous season's growth. Do not cut back to less than a minimum height of about 18 inches. Of course, some weak-growing bushes may require a lower minimum height in order to develop the bush properly. To explain: Cut back a 60-inch growth to 30 inches, a 40-inch growth to 20 inches, and so on.

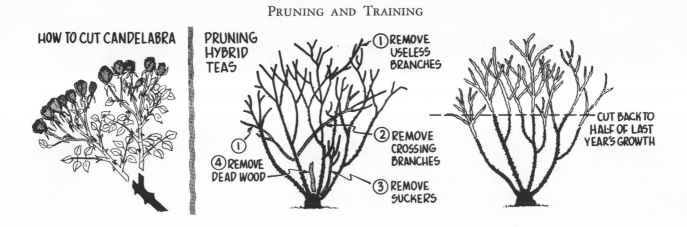

As you learn the growing habits of your different roses, you may want to alter this rule in the case of specific varieties. You may want to cut some very strong growers back less, some weak growers more. No one pruning rule can apply to all varieties. In all cases be careful and conservative in your pruning.

1. To start your pruning, remove all dead or unhealthy canes. Take them off with a clean saw cut, flush with the bud union.

2. Remove all useless small branches and twiggy growth. Then evaluate the remaining canes. If there are more than five, remove one or more of the older canes that have become hard, knotty, poor producers of blooms. You can usually remove at least one old cane each year, cutting it off at its base. On a healthy, vigorous bush, one or more new replacement shoots can be expected each growing season. The newer canes can be identified by their lighter green color. The most and best flowers grow on the newer wood. However, do not remove old wood needed to give a well balanced symmetry to your bush. One-sided bushes make a poor appearance and often yield a poor production of blooms.

3. Remove branches that cross over the center. In fact, it is always well to keep the center open to light and circulation of air.

4. Next, study the terminal or upper lateral branching growth. Cut back all strong side branches to the third or fourth eye. It is this terminal growth which usually will produce the first crop of good flowers.

Varieties with a naturally upright growth should be cut to an outside bud to spread the growth. Sprawling varieties can be pruned to an inside bud in order to make them grow more upright.

PRUNING FLORIBUNDA ROSES

In pruning floribundas, remember that the floribunda is a different type of rose than the hybrid tea and serves a different purpose in the garden. It is essentially a flowering shrub, beautiful for its mass of rich color rather than its individual blooms.

1. Prune for pleasing, well balanced form, and for uniform height if the bush is used in a hedge, border, or massed color bed.

2. Keep all of the good, flower-producing canes. Remove any dead or useless wood, and remove spent clusters of flowers by cutting back to a strong bud.

3. The floribunda should be cut back about one-fourth of its previous year's growth. This should remove most of the small, twiggy top growth. Shape the plant as you prune.

4. If strong, ambitious canes shoot up above the bush and spoil the symmetrical appearance, these can be cut back to the desired height after they have finished blooming. If this growth does not look out of place, let it remain and bloom as it will.

PRUNING GRANDIFLORA ROSES

Grandifloras, vigorous growers with strong canes, should be pruned about the same as hybrid teas. Cut back to one-half of the previous season's growth.

PRUNING RAMBLER ROSES

The ramblers produce many long, vigorous basal canes each year. These canes produce the flowers of the following year, blooming only once each year in the early summer.

Prune just after their blooming period is finished. Remove all canes that have flowered by severing with a clean cut at the base of the cane. The old woods rarely bloom again, so do not retain them. Save their space and the plant vigor they use up to force new canes.

Examples: DOROTHY PERKINS, BLOOMFIELD COURAGE, CRIMSON RAMBLER.

PRUNING CLIMBERS AND HYBRID TEA RAMBLERS

REMOVE FADED FLOWERS. CUT STEMS AT STRONG BUD BENEATH FLOWER LEAVING 2-3 LEAF BUDS

REMOVE OLD CANE AT BUD UNION

TRAIN PRUNED CLIMBER IN ARCHED POSITION AND TIE IN PLACE

PRUNING LARGE-FLOWERED CLIMBERS

These natural climbers have habits of growth and blooming similar to ramblers but display larger flowers in handsome clusters.

Blooms are produced on canes developed the previous year.

Their blooming habits vary according to varieties.

While this class of climbers is generally credited with blooming only once in each summer season, several of the varieties are known to repeat rather generously.

This repetition is encouraged by mild climatic conditions with generous feeding and watering.

Notable among these possible repeaters are Dr. W. Van Fleet, Paul's Scarlet, Belle of Portugal, Mary Wallace, Mme. Gregoire Staechelin, Kitty Kininmonth, and others according to growing conditions.

These "large-flowered climbers" have a widely differing ancestry and hence have varied habits of growth and production. Until you know your plants, you should exercise careful judgment and restraint in pruning this class.

Retain some of the canes that have just flowered along with the new canes that have grown up in the current season. About 2 of each is a good average. Many varieties of this class will flower on laterals coming from the older canes retained. Each season remove one or more of the oldest basal canes, your aim being to retain a total of not more than 4. This is as many as the roots can nourish properly.

To finish, thin out any weak non-contributing branches in the foliage area. Cut back the remaining lateral or side branches to 2 or 3 leaf buds.

Keep in mind always the symmetrically balanced appearance of your plants. Much can be done to prune and train your climbers to form a well planned pattern of colorful beauty. Climbers are grown for display, not for cut flowers.

With this class of natural climbers, little good is accomplished by removing the seed pods or hips which follow the blooms. In fact, many varieties will not produce their second crop of flowers if the old spent flower clusters are removed. The newer secondary blooms seem to come from the midst of the old clusters or from immediately below them, probably from delayed flower buds. Also, there is decorative beauty in the colorful seed hips of many varieties, such as Mme. Gregoire Staechelin, Paul's Lemon Pillar, and Belle of Portugal.

PRUNING EVERBLOOMING CLIMBERS

It is really a misnomer to term any of this group "everblooming." They generally do produce flowers in some quantities rather continuously throughout the flowering season. In most cases, however, the mature plants produce a great burst of blooms early in the season and then flower with more or less quantity and regularity throughout the balance of the year. Often there is one comparatively large burst of blooms in the fall.

1. Climbing Hybrid Teas

The majority of the climbing roses produced today belong to this extensive class of modern roses. With a few exceptions, they are mutations or sports of bush roses and usually bear the name of the bush rose from which they originated.

(a) *Newly planted hybrid tea climbers* should be left unpruned until they have achieved two or three years' growth after planting. It takes that long for them to mature and attain good size and satisfactory flower production. Do not cut back; merely remove all dead canes and branches and any twiggy useless growth.

Shape your plants as they grow, to give them the pleasing form and symmetry desirable when they have attained maturity.

(b) *Mature hybrid tea climbers* are ready for their first annual pruning after two or three years of normal growth.

Prune them at the same time you do your hybrid tea bushes, at the end of the dormant period. Limit the number of main upright canes on a mature plant to 2 or 3 of the youngest and most vigorous.

New basal canes will come up each year on a healthy hybrid tea climber. At each pruning period, remove as many of the oldest canes as are necessary to reduce the total number to the 2 or 3 desired.

Very little pruning of hybrid tea climbers is necessary or desirable. The aim should be to develop and retain as many of the flower-bearing laterals and sub-laterals (side branches) as possible. Cut back the tops of the main upright canes lightly, if necessary, to control their growth. Treat the large upright-growing side branches in the same manner.

Remove entirely any branches that extend outward in a manner to spoil the symmetrical appearance of the plant.

Cut back to 2 or 3 bud eyes all of the smaller side branches which will bear your flowers.

Hybrid tea climbers bloom rather sparingly on very new wood. The best blooms are produced on short spur branches growing out of two or three-year-old canes.

(c) *During the flowering season,* remove all spent blooms promptly. Cut back the branches on which they have flowered to a strong bud two or three bud eyes from a main stem.

Note instructions on training climbers. These will supplement your rules for pruning. Proper training will greatly increase the number of flowers.

2. *Climbing Floribundas and Polyanthas*

Prune mature plants of this class just as you do hybrid tea climbers. Thin out and shape the growing plants in order that they may attain a well balanced decorative form when they are mature.

You can retain 4 or 5 main upright canes on plants of this class.

Remove all spent blooms promptly during the flowering season to encourage repeat blooming. Cut them off at the first strong bud eye below the cluster being removed.

Examples: CLIMBING PINOCCHIO, CLIMBING GOLDI-LOCKS, CLIMBING FLORADORA, CLIMBING CECILE BRUNNER, CLIMBING GLORIA MUNDI.

3. *Everblooming (Natural) Climbers*

Like the hybrid teas, these so-called "everblooming" climbers, have a profuse main blooming period in late spring and early summer with persistent intermittent blooming through the balance of the summer and fall. Many of the varieties in this class, such as NEW DAWN, DR. J. H. NICOLAS, so closely resemble hybrid tea climbers in appearance and growth habits that they usually are classed as such.

By reason of their varied genetic ancestry and growth habit, no set pruning rule would apply to all of this class.

In general, prune them conservatively just as you would hybrid tea climbers, at least until you learn their growth and flowering habits and feel that they require a different treatment.

MERMAID, as one exception, needs no pruning except possibly to restrain its wild growth. Merely remove dead and useless canes and branches.

Pillars

Most typical pillar climbers belong in this class. While often grown spread out and displayed like other climbers, their greatest beauty is shown when they are grown and trimmed as pillars of flowers.

Climbers trained for such display are lightly thinned out and cut back to maintain the characteristic symmetry of the pillar form. Remove all dead and useless branches. Cut back all side branches that have flowered to 2 or 3 bud eyes from main stems. Remove all spent blooms promptly when noted, and cut back the side branches on which they have flowered.

Pruning rose pillars properly is a matter of observation and experience. They are well worth any care required. A carefully maintained rose pillar can be one of the most beautiful features in your garden.

TRAINING OF CLIMBING ROSES

Climbers can be trained in such a manner as to increase greatly their production of flowers as well as to enhance the beauty of their display.

When the vertical canes have grown to a sufficient height, say 8 to 10 feet, spread them out at an angle from their base, spacing them evenly. Arch all of these long verticals with the ends tied and pointing downward.

Through an interesting natural phenomenon, this arching will cause each leaf bud along the upper side of

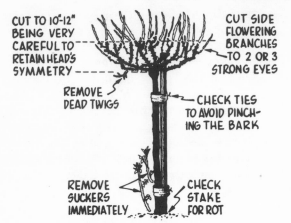

CUT TO 10"-12" BEING VERY CAREFUL TO RETAIN HEAD'S SYMMETRY

CUT SIDE FLOWERING BRANCHES TO 2 OR 3 STRONG EYES

REMOVE DEAD TWIGS

CHECK TIES TO AVOID PINCHING THE BARK

REMOVE SUCKERS IMMEDIATELY

CHECK STAKE FOR ROT

How to prune tree roses

the arched canes to push out shoots and produce one or more flowers. This method of training will increase flower production to a very marked degree.

To explain this phenomenon: The cane of a rose, placed in an upright position, will draw on the supply of the carbohydrates in the plant, chiefly to build new tissues and increase the upward growth of the plant. When this same cane is placed in a horizontal or arched position, the utilization of the carbohydrates for upward growth is checked and a greater percentage of this necessary plant food remains available for the development of flowering shoots and their blooms.

After flowering, remove all spent blooms with a clean cut at the first well developed leaf bud below them.

Climbers on a fence or wall should be trained in a similar manner. They can be tied in an arched or horizontal position. If the last 12 inches or so of the extended canes is bent and tied pointing downward, the blooming performance will be greatly increased, as with the tall-growing climbers.

PRUNING TREE ROSES

Standard or tree roses have a more formal decorative value than the same varieties do in bush form. A great deal of their beauty lies in the spread and shapeliness of their flowering heads. This beauty must be maintained by studied care in the pruning and seasonal trimming.

Tree roses should be cut back very carefully with the objective of having an evenly balanced symmetrical head of foliage and flowers during the blooming period.

Be certain that you use very sharp pruning shears or knife to avoid any damage and dieback of the canes. You cannot afford to lose any.

As a particular reason for care in pruning, bear in mind always that standards do not produce as much new

growth from the bud union as bush roses, particularly after four or five years' growth. Be chary about cutting away main branches even of the older wood, for you can easily unbalance a head and destroy its beauty.

Keep in mind the shaping of the head when you cut flowers or remove spent blooms.

1. To prune, first remove all dead, twiggy and useless wood.

2. Then cut back the main branches to a length of 10 to 12 inches. The length of the cut-back branches should be approximately the same on all sides so as to maintain a symmetrical balance. All exceptionally tall or widespread branches should be cut back in proportion to the general dimensions and form of the head.

3. Cut back lateral or side-flowering branches to 2 or 3 strong bud eyes.

4. When you have finished pruning a standard, check the stake to which it is tied. See if it has rotted below ground, then check all of the ties to see if they are holding properly and not pinching the bark. Be sure that the wires of plant labels are not cutting into the stem or branches—tight wires have killed many fine standards.

5. Remove any sucker that appears either along the trunk or from the root stock.

PRUNING OLD-FASHIONED ROSES, SHRUB ROSES, HYBRID PERPETUALS

The three groups listed above represent a varied collection of roses from other days—the roses of our ancestors. Few growers handle these roses today.

A great number of different species and hybrids are included, representing many diverse rose families. Most of them are vigorous growers, develop into large bushes which need only thinning and shaping with very little actual cutting back.

No general pruning rule can cover all of these many species and rose families. Until the rose grower has learned the habits and characteristics of each specific variety, he would be wise to prune them lightly.

Shape the bushes by cutting back any overly long shoots to the general pattern of the plant. If the bush has grown too big for its location, remove entirely some of the oldest main canes. Prune the flowering branches lightly.

As most of these large bushes are used for landscaping, hedges, and specimens, the primary pruning effort should be to trim and shape them to fit their place in the landscape picture.

CHAPTER NINE

Winter Protection

Roses are unquestionably hardy plants. They show a remarkable ability to tolerate severe winter conditions in various parts of the country. However, this tolerance differs with the type and variety of rose and with the severity of the winter temperatures.

Generally speaking, all bush and climbing roses including floribundas will stand temperatures down to 10° F. without protection. Tree roses should be protected against temperatures below 15°. Shrub and old-fashioned roses are hardier and will need winter protection only in areas where temperatures drop to −10°.

Winter climates vary so greatly that it is a wise practice to get local advice on protection requirements for your particular area. The American Rose Society has a Consulting Rosarian in your region. His advice is at your service with no charge whatsoever. For his name and address write to the American Rose Society, 4048 Roselea Place, Columbus 14, Ohio. If there is no Consulting Rosarian in your locality, check with your nursery or your County Agent.

In practically all areas where roses are garden grown, if the roots are properly protected, the bushes will usually escape unscathed. The damage to roots and canes that accumulates from the alternate thawing and freezing of those parts can be especially harmful. But if you insulate the roots properly, you will rarely lose a bush. If the roots survive the winter, the tops will grow again. This is not true of standard roses which require special protection (see below).

WHAT TO USE

It is generally agreed that the best winter protection for roses of all types is to mound them up at their bases with a covering of friable soil that will drain easily and not hold moisture against the canes. Mound this covering up around the canes to a height of 10 to 12 inches, and maintain it at that height throughout the winter.

Bring in this covering soil from outside your garden or from a plant-free area of your yard. Do not scrape it up from the soil around your roses and thus expose thinly covered roots to frost damage.

Avoid covering the bushes with manure, leaves, grass cuttings, or similar materials that would remain a wet, soggy, rotting mass around the canes. Such an unhealthful condition can kill as many roses as frost. Avoid any type of covering that will keep the canes continually moist or wet. Dense clay soil, such as adobe, retains moisture too long to be satisfactory for packing around the bush.

Many good gardeners put evergreen boughs or straw over the soil mounds. This acts as a windbreak, keeps the soil in place, and does no injury.

Before applying the protective covering to your bush roses, cut back the tops to a height of about 3 feet, and remove the leaves. This will lessen the possibility of their being whipped about by winter winds which might disturb the mounding protection.

A bush that has grown with health and vigor throughout the past season will stand severe cold much better than one of weak growth.

TREE ROSES

Tree roses (standards) require special protective treatment because they will not stand quite as low temperatures as bush roses.

To be safely protected, they must be laid over on their sides, with the heads sunk at least halfway in a shallow trench, and mounded up with friable soil as advised for bush roses.

To do this: Cut back the branches of the head to 10 or 12 inches and loosen the roots, on one side only, by digging under and around them. Now, bend the standard over on its side to ground level, with head in shallow trench stake it down, and mound up roots, stem, and top as advised for bush roses. It is well to have the mound cover all branches of the head because this growth is easily hurt by frost. Finish with a topping of evergreen boughs or straw.

When killing frosts are over in the spring, uncover the bush, stand it up in place, and re-cover the exposed roots with prepared planting soil. When you uncover the tops, do so with care in order not to break off any shoots that have made an early start.

CLIMBING ROSES

The majority of climbers today are hybrid teas which are sensitive to temperatures below 10° F. If they are fastened to buildings and fences that provide protection from cold dry winds, they will often weather temperatures down to zero or even a bit below.

In areas where temperatures are at all liable to go below 10° F, it is wise to protect the roots from killing frosts even if the tops are exposed. Mound up the base of your climbers with soil, to 12 or 14 inches, as you do your bush roses.

In areas of extreme, below-zero temperatures it will be necessary to remove the climbers from their wall or framework supports. In the fall when the tip growth is pliant, lay them out on the ground and pin them down

in place. Mound the recumbent canes with a soil covering and with evergreen branches or straw.

WHEN TO APPLY PROTECTIVE MATERIALS

As to the time for applying needed protection, be on the safe side and finish your covering the first two weeks in November.

The first freezing blasts of north wind usually come about the middle of November, but they could come roaring down earlier.

REMOVING PROTECTIVE MOUNDS IN SPRING

In early spring, when the normal period of sudden freezes is over, remove the mounding soil and other coverings from all of your roses of all types. Keep it nearby, however, to use in case of an unseasonable frost.

Remove carefully, in order not to break off any young shoots that have started.

When you prune the uncovered bushes, look for frost damage and cut back below it. Frost damage is indicated by brown spots inside the center, or pith, of the cane. Shorten the stem gradually, snip by snip, until brown spots or signs of discoloration are no longer visible.

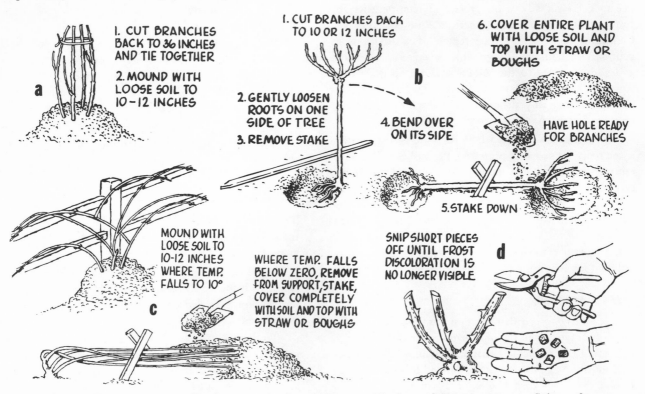

WINTER PROTECTION: a. Bush roses; b. Standards; c. Climbers; d. How to prune off frost damage

CHAPTER TEN

How to Grow Roses in Containers

The rose is not ordinarily regarded as a good container plant, yet if you are willing to devote time to their care, roses can be grown quite successfully in redwood boxes, or in tubs and pots.

Roses flower more heavily over a longer period of time than most other shrubs that are popularly grown in containers. Their exotic reds, oranges, yellow, and softer pastel shades show off handsomely against a wall or a mass of evergreen shrubs or as ornaments to a patio or lanai. When planted in containers, roses can be moved about wherever you need color most; and the plants can be retired from sight during their dormant period.

Roses in containers do present their problems, however. Many gardeners who have tried this planting idea give up after a season or two. Where summers are hot and the air is dry—away from the coast—roses dry out very quickly and require constant watering. When grown in this manner, they require more care than if grown in the garden.

WHICH TYPES CAN BE USED

As a general rule, the polyanthas and floribundas are best adapted to container culture because of their bushy compact growth, moderate height and the fact that they bloom almost continuously throughout the greater part of the rose season. Their cluster-blooming habit affords a generous spread of color that adds to their charm.

Hybrid teas with their larger bushes are not so satisfactory for container growing as the floribundas. They are apt to grow tall and rather top heavy, particularly in mild climates; and their bloom is more intermittent.

Three good polyanthas for container work are THE FAIRY, MARGO KOSTER, and PERLE D'OR.

Nearly all of the floribundas will make good container plants. Particularly to be recommended are BABY BLAZE, PINOCCHIO, LILIBET, FASHION, RED WONDER, ROSENELFE, RED PINOCCHIO, IRENE OF DENMARK, JIMINY CRICKET, PINKIE, CHINA DOLL.

KINDS AND SIZES OF CONTAINERS

Containers for roses should be large enough to hold an ample amount of soil with some free space at the top for watering.

The square redwood box makes the best container. These are obtainable at most garden supply shops or by mail order in a great variety of kinds and sizes, plain and ornamental. The round tubs are not so practical. They provide less space for roots and, having a small round base, blow over rather easily.

Your box container should have slats on the bottom to insure good drainage and air circulation underneath. They should have 5, ½-inch drainage holes distributed about the bottom.

As to size, the 12-inch square container is suitable for low growers of moderate size such as PINKIE, CHINA DOLL, and MARGO KOSTER. The 14-inch square box will accommodate the larger floribundas; a 16-inch square box is not too large but it is quite heavy when filled with damp soil.

Clay pots can be used; but they are heavy and very easily broken, and they are inclined to blow over in a wind. Clay pots should be painted inside with a clear black roofing paint to lessen the drying out of the root areas by evaporation through the sides of the pot.

HOW TO PLANT

Container-grown roses require good soil. A tested planting mixture, recommended by the San Mateo County Rose Society, is made up as follows:

7 parts good, loose garden loam
1 part peat moss

1½ parts well rotted cow manure

½ part alfalfa meal (can be omitted if not available) We would add to this mixture a generous portion of bone meal, say a 6-inch pot to the approximate wheelbarrow load of the mixture. A bit more or less will make no difference.

This material should be put together and well mixed 6 to 8 weeks before using to insure its being properly seasoned.

Before planting, prune the roots back to 8 or 10 inches. In planting they may have to be bent slightly to conform to the shape of the container, but they should not be coiled around each other. Place pieces of crock over the drainage holes and cover the bottom with about an inch of sphagnum moss (best) or pine needles pressed down over the bottom of the container. The moss or needles prevent soil from plugging up the drainage holes.

Fill container about one quarter full of the planting mixture. Place plant in the center, spread out the roots in a well balanced formation, and fill in around them with the prepared soil, firming it well about the roots and under the crown. When the plant is finally set, the bud union should be about an inch above the soil surface; and the soil level 2 inches below the rim of the container. Firm the soil down well, particularly around the sides of the container so that irrigation water will not run down between the soil and the container leaving the roots dry. A firmly packed soil allows the water to seep down slowly and to soak all parts of the root area.

WATERING AND FEEDING

Water only enough to keep all of the soil in the container moist but not overly wet. Never permit it to dry out and the plant to droop. This is a vital thing in container growing. Although daily watering may be required in very hot weather, watering every second or third day is usually adequate. Because constant watering takes all of the soluble nutrients from even the best soils, it is important to feed container roses regularly during the active growing period. Apply fertilizer about every two weeks after growth has started. A liquid fertilizer, such as fish emulsion, is best for container plants. It is easier to apply and, being in a liquid form, all of its nutrients become immediately available to the plant.

If you use a dry fertilizer, be sure that it is completely water soluble so that undissolved elements will not build up in the soil. Apply the dry fertilizer evenly, scratch it lightly into the soil surface, and water it in thoroughly.

MULCHING

A mulch keeps the surface roots cool and prevents excessive evaporation and drying out of the soil. The best mulch is cow or steer manure. For appearance's sake, this can be covered with a coating of small stone, coarse gravel or white marble chips. Small potted plants around the base of the bush can provide an attractive finish.

PLANT RENEWAL

It isn't necessary or practical to change the soil in large containers every year. Instead, remove a slice of soil from around the edge of the container each year when the plants are most dormant. With a sharp trowel, dig out the soil as deeply as possible in a band 1 to 3 inches wide around the edge of the tub. As you dig, be careful to cut, rather than tear out, any feeder roots growing in the upper surface. Then fill in the excavated portion with fresh soil and pack it firmly.

In smaller containers, roses should be handled like any other container plant. They should be knocked out each year, root-pruned, and replanted.

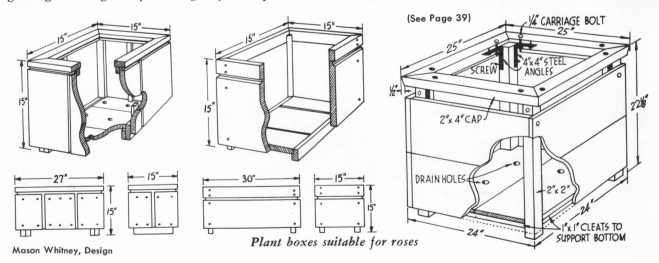

Mason Whitney, Design

Plant boxes suitable for roses

CHAPTER ELEVEN

Control of Diseases and Insect Pests

Roses are among the healthiest, most vigorous, and easiest to grow of all the garden flowers. A well grown plant will shake off pest attacks and diseases with minimum assistance from the spray gun.

Your first line of defense against pests in roses—or in any garden plant—must be in the health of the plant itself. No experienced gardener needs to be told that a sickly plant succumbs to pests much more quickly than a healthy one. A rose growing in part shade, pallid for want of sunlight, is much more apt to be seriously damaged by aphis than a plant growing vigorously in a warm, sunny corner of the garden.

Constant spraying won't make a healthy rose out of one which is sickly for reasons of climate, exposure, soil, or water. Sprays and dusts have one purpose: to control pests and disease. Wait until symptoms appear before applying control. Fungus disease is an exception. When symptoms appear the damage has been done. Preventive measures should be used when and where fungus is a problem. On these pages we list the pests that cause most of the rose troubles with their recommended controls.

In most areas, the Big Three—aphis, mildew, and spider mites—are more important than all the other rose pests and diseases together. Aphis affect roses everywhere while plants are in active growth. Mildew is a constant menace to a greater or lesser degree in all areas. It is particularly difficult in coastal areas. Mites are most serious in hot, dry, inland areas.

Yearly Program

A sound pest control program begins in winter, after plants are pruned. Remove and burn all old leaves at pruning time, and tidy up the ground around the rose bed.

With the beginning of leaf-out, in spring, start controls as soon as you see the first aphis, and repeat sprayings every week to keep up with new hatchings.

If and when mildew first appears on new growth, apply a recommended spray or one of the combination dusts containing sulfur plus other materials.

Mites may strike mature leaves during the first hot days of spring or summer. Tiny dots and larger yellow areas appear on upper sides of leaves; tiny webs and dark brown areas show on under sides. Miticides such as tedion, kelthane, or aramite will control mites; or use a combination spray which contains a miticide.

Pesticides

The modern science of horticultural chemistry has devised efficient all-purpose insecticides that alone will kill and control all major garden insect pests, and fungicidal materials that control common diseases of the rose.

Using the following basic materials, you can break down your attack according to the kind of insect pest or disease:

1. Malathion in combination with other insecticides and miticides for chewing or sucking insects. Alone it is not an efficient control of spider mites.

2. Sulfur (dusting or wettable) combined with other material, or liquid 26% calcium polysulfide (lime sulfur) for mildew.

3. PHALTAN® (Phthalimide fungicide), a wettable powder for control of the three main rose diseases: mildew, rose rust, and black spot.

SPRAYING VS. DUSTING

Each of these methods for applying pest control materials is widely used, and each has its merits.

The present trend seems to favor liquid spraying as against dusting. The highly effective new liquid chemical preparations plus new and better spray apparatus certainly favor liquid application.

Dusts, with their lasting residual coverages, do offer considerable protection if applied frequently and thoroughly in advance of infestation. However, when an insect pest or disease already has taken hold, spraying will usually bring the trouble under control more quickly and expeditiously.

SPRAYING EQUIPMENT

The mechanical means we employ for applying sprays and dusts are just as important as the materials which they apply.

The many types available should be considered from the point of view of the number of bushes to be sprayed and the nature of the work to be done. In general, buy a good applicator and keep it in a clean condition.

Whichever type you buy should apply the spray solution well atomized and with force and should be designed to permit efficient coverage of the undersides of the leaves.

Handiest for general use is the familiar hose-attachment sprayer, obtainable in several sizes for different garden requirements. This type of sprayer, very accurate and efficient, is a bottle arrangement that is attached as a nozzle to a garden hose and operated by its water pressure. Diluted spray material is measured into the bottle in accordance with instructions on the product label. Spray is metered through a needle valve into the hose stream and discharged in a fine spray through a nozzle on the bottle cap. The sizes recommended are the 2-gallon which will cover 10 to 15 rose bushes, and the 6-gallon which will spray 40-50 bushes. For spraying properly with a wettable powder, which keeps in suspension but does not dissolve, it is advisable to shake the spray bottle frequently to keep the powder in suspension and prevent clogging.

The small plunger-type sprayers of 1 or 2-quart capacity are hardly suitable for rose garden use. It is difficult to secure proper coverage with this type sprayer.

The better trombone-action sprayers, drawing suspended material solution from a pail, are efficient if the material is stirred well at least every 10 minutes. It takes muscle power to operate this type.

For larger gardens, up to about 200 bushes, the tank-type sprayer is recommended. These come in 2 to 4-gallon capacities, and can be pumped up to give good pressure. Some models come on wheels, similar to a golf bag cart. Choose only tanks with safety tops. Also, be sure there are 5 or 6 feet of hose for freedom of movement.

For very large gardens, a power sprayer operated by an electric or gasoline motor is desirable. These usually are mounted on rubber-tired wheels. They operate at a maintained hose pressure of over 100 pounds, and throw a finely atomized spray stream with great force and over a considerable area. With a power sprayer, one can cover 500 large bushes thoroughly in about two hours. The high pressure and consequent fine atomization of the spray means greater coverage with less material. When buying or making a power sprayer, be sure that it has a built-in agitator of some kind.

Spraying Routine

As important as good control materials and the practical mechanical spraying devices is efficient application.

1. Start your spraying program with the first appearance of insect pests or fungus diseases. Mildew and aphis usually will be the first to appear.

2. Maintain your program systematically throughout the growing season and keep a date record of your sprayings and the materials used.

3. Spray thoroughly, every 7 days. Be sure to cover both the upper surfaces and under surfaces of the leaves. Start at the base of each bush, working upward with a side-to-side rolling movement of the nozzle pipe. Try to cover the bottom of every leaf, for this area is the most vulnerable to insect and disease attack. By the time the top of the bush has been reached, the "rain-back" of the spray will have covered most of the leaf tops. A supplementary swish or two of spray over the tops usually will finish the coverage. Spray with force for the most satisfactory results.

4. Spray early in the morning to avoid sunburn on wet leaves. Use no form of sulfur spray or dust when garden temperatures rise above 85° at the point where the bush grows.

In climates where the spray would dry in an hour or two, evening spraying may work out fairly well. This is a matter for trial and observation.

5. To lessen possible leaf burn after spraying, tap or shake off the surplus of spray which has accumulated in cupped leaves and on the leaf points. A successful way to do this tapping-shaking, is to use two light bamboo plant sticks about 5 feet long, held in one hand with the ends approximately 10 inches apart. This tapping-shaking is an important finish to all spraying practice.

6. Irrigate your plants thoroughly the day before spraying, particularly if the soil is dry. Damp soil tends to shield the plant against leaf burn.

DUSTING APPARATUS

If you prefer dusting for pest control, and you expect worthwhile results, you will find a duster of high quality to be indispensable.

To get proper coverage, the dust must blow out with force and in an even flow which can be regulated by the operator. The dusting device should have a deflecting nozzle adjustment for under-leaf or over-leaf dusting. There are several medium priced, metal-plunger type dusters that work very efficiently.

For smoother operation and better coverage, bellows-type dusters or the rotary type are preferable. For large plantings, a knapsack blower with side lever action and continuous flow of dust under high pressure, or a rotary-type duster will give good results. One type of duster utilizes a small, crank-driven rotary fan that blows dust out with good force. See sketch "d" below.

Dusting Routine

Objectives and methods for dusting are similar to those for spraying: there must be full coverage on both the top and the bottom of the leaf. Avoid putting on too much dust, a common fault. A light, inconspicuous coverage is enough. If there is a noticeably heavy coating on the leaves, you have dusted too heavily.

Do your dusting when the air is still, and preferably when the leaves are dry. Even a slight breeze will blow the dust everywhere but on the rose on which it is intended to go. Morning or evening is usually the best dusting time.

ROSE DISEASES
Mildew

Powdery mildew is a common fungus disease of the rose, prevalent to a greater or lesser degree virtually wherever roses are grown. Nearly all types of roses will be affected by mildew if planted where conditions are favorable for its development; floribundas and grandifloras are fairly resistant; rambler roses very susceptible.

The disease appears as a grayish powdery growth on the leaves, stems and buds of roses. The newer, softer top growth usually is affected first. The infected leaves quickly become crumpled and distorted, an injury that is more or less of a permanent nature. The older leaves will also mildew, but less readily and with less injury.

Mildew is difficult to prevent, particularly in urban areas. The spores are widely circulated by air currents. Humidity of the air and rapid changes of temperature encourage the spread and germination of the mildew spores which alight on leaf, stem, and flower surfaces. These spores do not germinate on wet leaf surfaces.

Although mildew appears on roses in practically every area where they are grown, it thrives most freely and is most difficult to control in coastal areas, particularly where warm, damp, and foggy conditions prevail, or where there are rapid changes in temperature.

Control: Phaltan is a positive control for all three of the most bothersome diseases: mildew, rose rust, and black spot.

Best results are obtained by spraying every 7 or 8 days with 75% Phaltan. This is a wettable powder used at a strength of 1½ level tablespoons to the gallon of water. It contains an efficient wetting agent, and if you wish you can include in the solution any of the better insecticides for a single-action spraying. Apply this spray with force, thoroughly covering the entire plant. Take particular care to spray the undersides of the leaves. For maximum results, Phaltan should be used as a preventative, starting early in the growing season. While the spray normally leaves very little residue, it is highly advisable to remove

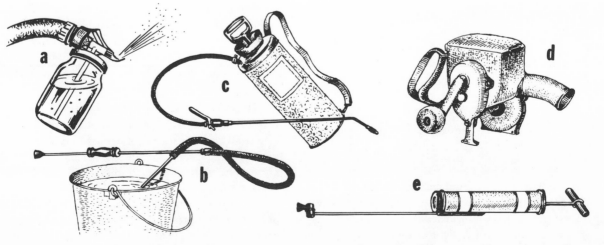

DEVICES FOR DUSTS AND SPRAYS: *a. Hose attachment for liquid controls. b. Trombone sprayer for liquid* *or wettable powder. c. Tank sprayer for large gardens. d. Rotary-type duster. e. Plunger-type duster*

surplus spray (see the tapping-shaking procedure, described under *Spraying Routine* on page 72). This cleaning action can be done quickly and easily, and is recommended when using any wettable powder spray.

Wettable sulfur sprays with a good spreader-sticker added are effective. Use at a dosage strength of 2 level tablespoons of wettable sulfur and ½ teaspoon of a mild detergent to a gallon of water. However, if temperatures rise to 85° or more at the point where the rose is growing, leaf burn is a probability with the use of any sulfur materials.

Sulfur dusts are relatively effective for mildew prevention if treatment is started early, but are not very useful when mildew has become established. Phaltan as a wettable powder is much more effective.

Formulations of copper derivatives, dusts and sprays, are favored in many regions, particularly in periods of high temperatures.

In coastal mildew areas, a year-round formulation of calcium polysulfide (lime sulfur) provides good control of mildew on roses and many other plants subject to the same vexing fungus trouble. Do not use the calcium polysulfide when temperatures in the garden are above 85°.

Rose Leaf Rust

This fungus disease of the rose leaf is quite prevalent on the Pacific Coast and in the Southwest and is occasionally found in eastern coastal areas. It can disfigure the foliage; if severe it can defoliate the plants.

Its appearance, usually in late spring, is first denoted by small bright orange spots on the undersides of the leaves. These spots enlarge and soon appear as yellow blotches on the upper sides.

The infection spreads, particularly with warm weather, forming thick powdery masses of orange spores on the undersides of the leaves.

These spores are easily shaken loose and widely distributed by air currents and rain. They germinate readily when they alight on a damp spot and penetrate the tissue of the leaf, setting up a new infestation. If not controlled, the rust infestation rapidly spreads and may defoliate your plants, reducing their vitality and flowering ability.

Control: The spray material containing 75% Phaltan wettable powder has proven to be an effective preventive control for rust. It is a clean material, doing little if any damage and disfigurement to the rose blooms. Apply as a spray at a formulation strength of 1½ level tablespoons to the gallon of water.

A wettable sulfur spray plus 10% of maneb or zineb generally affords a fair control for rust. Ferbam spray will give some control, but it stains leaves and flowers as well as paint on buildings and fences.

Start spraying for rust early in the spring when the new leaves are formed. Remove and destroy badly infected leaves when noted.

Black Spot

Black spot is definitely the most devastating of rose diseases. It is prevalent in most areas of this country; and wherever prevalent, it is difficult to control and prevent.

It is in areas having summer rains that the most persistent conditions of black spot infection are found. Rain not only is responsible for the spread of the infection but furnishes the wet leaf conditions necessary for its establishment in the leaf structure. Overhead sprinkling, if persistent, can duplicate these conditions and effects.

California and the warm semi-arid areas of the far West are practically free of this serious rose disease. However, even in California and other far western areas, persistent watering with overhead sprinklers does frequently bring on black spot.

This disease, as the name implies, is identified by black spots with irregular fringed margins appearing in quantity on the infected leaves and sometimes on the stems.

It is the result of a fungus disease infecting practically all varieties of roses, although some varieties are a bit more resistant to it than others. Varieties having a Pernetian parentage—usually roses of yellow, copper, and orange coloring—seem to be especially susceptible.

The tissue around the black spots may turn a bright yellow; and in the case of particularly susceptible varieties, the entire leaf may turn yellow and shortly drop off. In cases of serious infestation, the entire plant may defoliate, causing a serious loss of plant vigor and flowering ability.

The fungus is normally carried over the winter on old leaves rotting on the ground and in lesions in the canes. The spores germinate in the spring and are transmitted to young foliage by splashing rains or overhead sprinkling. The spores are not readily carried by air currents. If these spores alight on leaves that remain in a wet condition for 6 hours or more, they germinate, and the growing fungus penetrates the leaf structure. From these penetrations new black spots develop which produce great numbers of fresh spores to further extend the infection.

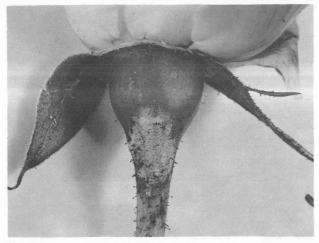

POWDERY MILDEW. *Evidenced by powdery white coating on buds, stems, leaves. New growth is affected first*

RUST. *First denoted by small orange spots on undersides of leaves. Yellow blotches appear on upper sides*

LEAFHOPPERS. *These sucking insects draw sap from the leaves, cause stippled appearance where they have fed*

APHIS. *Aphis badly damage tender new growth and slow plant's development. Leaves become distorted*

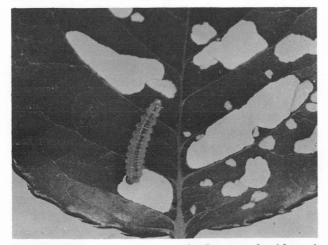

BRISTLY ROSE SLUG. *Larvae feed on undersides of leaves skeletonizing them between ribs or making holes*

LEAF CUTTING BEES. *Holes in leaves were made by leaf cutting bees which belong to same family as the sawfly*

Control: The most sensible and efficient control of this fungus disease always lies in timely measures for prevention of the disease. Of greatest importance is garden sanitation.

Keep the soil in your rose garden clear of fallen leaves and other decaying organic matter at all times. Promptly remove and destroy all such rubbish. This sanitary measure is of particular importance during the fall and winter seasons.

If there had been any black spot or rust infection on the foliage during the season past, the winter leaf carry-over would surely harbor it, and it would be transmitted to the new spring growth.

As an additional measure of protection, in the early spring after your seasonal pruning cut-backs, remove and destroy every leaf remaining on your rose bushes including those on your climbers.

As a final step in the post-winter cleanup, before the new growth starts, give your cut-back plants and the soil about them a thorough coverage of a dormant spray material. An excellent material for this dormant spraying is calcium polysulfide (lime sulfur) used at the strength recommended on the label for dormant season.

Dormant spraying with any recommended material should be completed before the buds start to break out and the new foliage growth begins. Otherwise the tender new growth might be damaged by any spray material used at "dormant strength."

For control of black spot in those areas of the country where it is most prevalent, 75% Phaltan will give excellent control. For best results, spray once a week regularly at a dosage strength of 1½ level tablespoons of Phaltan to a gallon of water.

Phaltan can also be combined with the calcium polysulfide or wettable sulfurs to make a complete spray for mildew and other fungus diseases of the rose.

Foliage should be protected by a coating of Phaltan during rainy periods in order to destroy the fungus spores as they germinate.

Sulfur as a dust or spray is moderately effective in some areas if combined with maneb or zineb, although most comparative tests made favor the efficiency of Phaltan for black spot control. Sulfur can cause excessive leaf burn when used in temperatures over 85° F. Ferbam will leave unsightly black deposits on leaves and flowers and may disfigure the paint on your buildings and fences. Sprays containing various forms of copper can cause red spotting and often cause defoliation, particularly in cool, damp weather.

Anthracnose

Anthracnose, a fungus leaf spot disease affecting rose plants, is reported occasionally from many parts of the country east and west. Its appearance is similar to that of black spot and it is very often confused with that disease.

The small circular spots are brownish at first, then develop a white center with reddish margins. The lesions, sometimes appearing on the canes, leave brown or purplish margins with depressed lighter centers.

Control: For most cases of proven anthracnose infection, the same spray control and methods of application recommended for black spot are advised.

Crown or Root Gall

This is a bacterial disease causing the abnormal growth of tumor-like swellings or galls on the crowns or the roots of roses.

The galls are irregular, globular bodies with convoluted surfaces, sometimes growing to diameters of several inches.

Control: If the galls noted are of small size, remove them completely with a sharp knife and paint the cut with a solution of household bleach in water or a mercuric fungicide, used per label instructions.

If the galls are large and cover a considerable area of the crown or roots, dig up and destroy the infected plant. A bush badly gall-infested is not worth saving.

Remove the soil in which the infected plant grew and replace it with clean soil before planting a new rose in the same location.

Brown Canker

This is a destructive fungus disease, usually identified in late winter or early spring by distinct patches of brown on the canes.

These brown patches result from the germination of canker spores the previous year, and from the penetration of the developed fungus into the structure of the canes.

The initial development of the canker infection during the summer season can be noted by the appearance of small purple-tinged or white spots on the canes. These enlarge and develop in the late winter or spring into the typical brown patches.

Infected canes can produce only poor, weak growth and blooms above the canker areas. The disease may destroy one or more canes, and, in fact, the entire plant.

Freezing of the bark on roses shipped in winter often brings on canker trouble.

Control: Cut out and burn all infected parts of the diseased plants. Make the cuts well below the diseased sections of the canes. Sterilize the pruning shears before each cut is made in order not to spread the infection into healthy wood. Sterilize the shears with household disinfectant, rubbing alcohol, or a garden fungicide.

For additional control, spray your rose plants with a dormant formula of liquid calcium polysulfide before new growth starts in the spring.

INSECT PESTS
Ants

Ants do not in themselves injure rose plants but they foster aphis and mealy bugs in the plants. They often dig nests around the roots. A spray composed of wettable chlordane in water or chlordane dust gives excellent ant control.

Aphis

The most prevalent insect pest in rose gardens everywhere is the aphis or plant louse. This is a small, soft-bodied insect, green, brown or red in color.

It appears very early in the spring, and multiplies with great rapidity. Aphis congregate in profusion on the new, succulent tip growth of leaves and buds. If the infestation is severe, malformation of the foliage, stems, and buds occurs, with definite damage to tender new growth and a slowing up of the plant's development.

Control: Good aphis control will result from timely spraying with effective materials when infestations first appear. Follow this treatment with two or more repeat applications at intervals of 7 days. Spraying will generally afford quicker and more positive control of aphis than dusting.

Particularly effective are the spray formulations containing lindane, DDT, and malathion; or rotenone and pyrethrum.

European Earwig

This is one of the most stubborn and disturbing insect pests to invade our homes and gardens. This variety of earwig is a European immigrant. It is found in the South and in the Pacific Coast areas, and has spread inland from the latter.

The European earwig is a dark brown insect about $5/8$ to 1 inch long with a pair of pincers on the rear end of its body. It feeds at night, and during the day it is found under rocks, boards, rubbish piles and in crevices. It voraciously attacks fruit, vegetables, leaves and flowers.

The earwig likes to work into the petal structure of the rose, eating holes in the petals and the leaves.

It usually lays its eggs in the soil, in winter, from December through February. The eggs hatch in early spring, and the hungry adults and young are very destructive, mainly in the period from April through early August.

Control: Poison baits, sprays, and dusts are all effective control methods. The best bait is a poisoned apple material scattered over areas which the pests frequent. Scatter the baits in the evening for best results. Bran baits are efficient, but must be kept away from animals.

Sprays containing chlordane or dieldrin, and the lindane-DDT-malathion combinations are very effective when applied thoroughly around woodpiles, fences, and the foundations of houses and out-buildings.

Dusts containing 1 to 2% lindane, or 5 to 10% of chlordane or DDT are also effectively used around buildings, fences, lumber piles and wherever the pests are found.

You may find it necessary to use all three—baits, sprays and dusts—to achieve a close control.

Fuller's Rose Beetle

Adult Fuller's rose beetles are moderately large with a short and broad snout. They are grayish in color with an oblique whitish line on each wing. This pest is closely related to the brachyrhinus "beetle," so destructive to camellias and rhododendrons.

They hide in the foliage in daytime and chew on the leaves at night. The eggs are laid near the tips of branches or near the base of the plant. The emerging grubs feed on the rootlets. This common pest is particularly destructive to roses.

Control: Poisoned apple bait scattered about the base of the plant is an effective killer.

Spray the plant heavily, covering its base and the soil around it with the malathion-DDT-lindane combination, or with dieldrin, saturating the soil for two or more inches down. Saturating in this manner kills the grubs as well as the beetles.

Grasshoppers

The grasshopper is a well known garden pest throughout the world. Young and adult hoppers attack any and all garden plants. If infestations are severe, great damage can result.

Control: For control, use poisoned baits scattered over infested areas, and use them repeatedly.

Dusts containing chlordane, DDT or lindane, have an efficient killing power.

Greenhouse Rose-Leaf Tier

The leaf tier belongs to a group of smooth caterpillars that feed heavily on garden plants. Pale in color, about 3/4 of an inch long, they are generally found within leaves which they have folded over or tied together.

When young, these caterpillars feed on the undersides of the leaves, and as they grow larger, they eat holes in the leaves.

Control: Hand-pick the infested leaves, or spray the foliage with the lindane-DDT-malathion combination, wettable DDT, or lindane wettable powder. Multi-purpose dusts also give good control.

Japanese Beetle

This most devastating pest has been confined, thus far, mostly to the central Atlantic areas. In early summer, heavy infestations, unless controlled, will voraciously attack the rose garden. They will strip the bushes of all buds, flowers, and young foliage within a few days. Their depredations continue until the frosts of autumn drive the pests underground.

The Japanese beetle is about 1/2 inch long, bright shining green with bronze or reddish wing covers. The larva is a white grub. One generation a year appears, coming up from the soil during late June and remaining until autumn frosts. The period of the greatest infestation is from July to early August. The eggs, laid in the soil during these warm summer months, hatch in 12 days, and the grubs feed on the roots of grass and smaller plants.

Control: All plants in affected areas must be protected against the swarms of Japanese beetles by the use of dusts and sprays.

The hoards of these pests can also be reduced by the use of traps and by industrious hand-picking.

Fair control, while difficult, is possible if the residents of an affected area will combine to put up a vigorous fight against the pests. This fight, to be successful, must be timely and thorough.

For control materials, lead arsenate and hydrated lime commonly are used.

The combination lindane-DDT-malathion spray has proved to be very effective in gaining control over this insect pest.

It is well to consult the state or county agricultural services of the area in which you garden, for these experts are usually able to render you valuable service in Japanese beetle control.

Leafhoppers

The leafhopper does little injury to the rose leaves on which it feeds, but it is an unsightly nuisance and a disturbance to the careful rose grower.

It is a diminutive hopper, a sucking insect, which feeds on the undersides of the leaves. The upper side of the leaf on which it has fed develops a stippled appearance from lighter colored spots where the hopper withdrew sap.

Control: Any good contact spray such as the lindane-DDT-malathion formulation or a DDT spray or dust will control the "hopper" pest.

Raspberry Cane Borer—Raspberry Horntail

This pest is a member of the sawfly family (see also page 80), common usually in the warmer coastal areas where it is a very destructive nuisance.

The adult sawflies are wasp-like insects about 1/2 inch in length, all black or black marked with yellow or orange.

In the larval stage, the sawfly closely resembles a caterpillar. The larvae measure about 1/2 inch in length.

The eggs are laid in punctures in the stem tissues. When the larvae hatch, they usually bore down through the pith of the stem. The stem so affected can be expected to droop above the puncture point and wilt.

Control: For efficient control, use lindane-DDT-malathion spray or wettable lindane powder or wettable DDT powder. These insecticides are applied to the upper half of the plant periodically throughout the growing season, after the first infestation is noted.

Red-Spider Mite

This tiny mite, very difficult to detect and control, is, in most areas, the most baffling and damaging pest with which the rose gardener has to contend.

This insect, not a spider and rarely red despite its name, is so small and inconspicuous that it is hardly visible to the naked eye. It is a tiny, eight-legged mite, oval in shape, with sucking mouth parts. Full grown, the red-spider mite is barely 1/60 of an inch in length and is usually a pale yellow color with two dark spots on its body. These spots give it the common name, "Two-Spotted Spider Mite."

Spider mites congregate almost entirely on the undersides of leaves where they may spin tiny white webs. It is on this underside where they breed and where the damage is done.

Spider mites are a warm-weather problem, as their colonies increase with greatest rapidity during periods of warm to hot weather. The mite lays many more eggs at the higher temperatures. It also follows that the higher

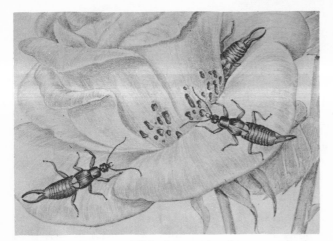

EUROPEAN EARWIG. *This destructive insect works into petal structure, eats holes in petals and leaves*

FULLER'S ROSE BEETLE. *Beetles work at night, chew notches in leaves. Larvae feed on roots of plants*

temperatures greatly accelerate the mite's development from egg to adult.

In action, mites suck the cell sap from the surface tissues of the leaves which in turn lose their green color and change to a yellow or bronzy cast. Soon after a mite attack, the underside of the leaf turns to a pale brown, speckled with white dots and white masses of webbing.

Shortly, from continued damage, the leaves may drop off. In aggravated cases, there can be complete defoliation of the plant in a brief time with consequent damage.

The best way to detect mites with certainty is to make frequent examinations of your plants, being on the alert for leaves showing any suspicious yellowing of the upper surfaces. Note particularly the leaves low down on the bushes, because these are the ones usually affected first.

Hold the leaves in the sunlight and examine them with a magnifying or reading glass. If mites are present, they will readily be observed, scuttling about on the under surface.

Control: Timeliness is the key. Get at the mites early and keep after them. Most of the oldest types of insecticides are of little use in mite eradication. However, a safe and effective remedy for most types of mites is found in sprays containing malathion and one of the new and very efficient miticides such as tedion.

One effective material, easily obtained, is the lindane-DDT-malathion-tedion formulation. It will give control over practically all insects and mites. In this combination the malathion kills the adult mites while the tedion works on the younger mites and the eggs. Use the above combination at the strength of two to three teaspoons, plus ¼ teaspoon of a mild detergent for a spreader, to each gallon of water.

For a really effective mite cleanup, you should spray twice at intervals of 7 days. The first spraying kills the adult mites, the second application is timed to kill mites hatching from eggs existing at the time of the first spraying. This second treatment kills them before they become mature and lay additional eggs. Spray very thoroughly, giving particular attention to the undersides of the leaves.

Most careful gardeners apply several sprayings at the same 7-day intervals, to insure complete cleanup of mites missed by the previous applications.

Rose Midge

This is a tiny but dangerous insect pest, which to date has not invaded the Pacific coastal areas. Its movement seems to have come no farther then the Rocky Mountain states.

The adult midge is a very minute fly, whose tiny light-colored maggots cause excessive damage to plants and blooms.

The rose midge usually appears in the early blooming period and lays its eggs in the tissues of the bud stems, causing them to bend over at right angles. The affected buds are blasted, the ruined tips of the shoots die, flowering practically ceases, and the upward growth of the plant is stopped.

Control: Spray or dust with DDT to provide an efficient control.

Early in the spring, when the rose growth is just starting, apply freely a water spray of DDT wettable powder to all of the soil areas of your rose garden. Use it at a strength of ¾ of an ounce to the gallon of water.

When flower buds first appear, spray the plants thoroughly with a lindane-DDT-malathion combination or with liquid DDT. Apply three times at 7-day intervals.

This treatment should afford good midge control, but it is wise to repeat the spraying frequently during the flowering season.

Rose Slugs—Sawflies (See also Raspberry Cane Borer)

When we speak of bristly rose slugs, cane borers, measuring worms, leaf worms, rose caterpillars, etc., we are usually referring to the larvae of one of several species of sawfly. The rose sawfly is one of several species of wasp-like insects that deposit their eggs in holes they have bored into the ends of a cut cane or branch, into stems of the flowers, or into slits they saw in the leaves. When the larvae hatch, they feed on the undersides of the leaves, skeletonizing them between the ribs, or making large holes through them. They can do a great deal of damage to the foliage of your roses, particularly to the climbers.

Control: The injury they cause can be easily prevented by an early-season spraying or dusting with such stomach poisons as the lindane-DDT-malathion formulations, DDT, or rotenone-pyrethrum sprays or dusts. Spray or dust so as to cover the undersides of the leaves.

Scale

Scale are sucking insects of several varieties, mostly small, and varying considerably in form and general appearance. Some show as dots of gray or brown on the canes and branches of the rose. Others resemble tiny oyster shells or have a cottony or waxy covering.

These insects in heavy infestation can do considerable damage, sucking out the juices of the plant and impairing its vigor. Often a main cane will die from the damage done by masses of scale.

Control: The best scale control is afforded during the winter clean-up season when stronger, more effective spray materials can be used without danger of foliage damage. Horticultural oil sprays are most effective.

If infestation is severe, use a spray combination composed of 5 tablespoons of oil spray with 1 tablespoon of the lindane-DDT-malathion formulation to each gallon of water. The oil cuts the waxy covering of the scale. Use this stronger formulation only in the dormant season.

Thrips

Thrips is another troublesome rose pest, found almost every place where roses are grown. This is a very tiny, slender insect of the sucking type, gray to black in color. It is about 1/20 of an inch long and has two pairs of fringed wings. Small as they are, thrips cause considerable damage to roses and to many other plants. Their rasping and puncturing of the flower surfaces cause discoloration and disfiguration, then these damaged surfaces become dry and deformed.

Thrips attack buds in their early stages, working their way in among the unfolded petals. If the infestations are severe, the buds turn brown, after which they often become misshapen, develop a tendency to "ball," and fail to open properly. Thrips frequently feed on the foliage and are found most often in the blooms of the lighter rather than the darker colors. Their presence is detected easily by examining the inner petals of a rose flower near the base of the petals.

Control: Thrips control may be accomplished by timely spraying, early in the season, with the arrival of the first warm weather. Good spray control materials are the lindane-DDT-malathion combination, and DDT. Multipurpose insecticide dusts are also effective in the control of thrips. Repeat applications of sprays or dusts.

Whiteflies

The whitefly is a pest of minor importance from the standpoint of the injury it inflicts, but it is an unsightly garden nuisance.

The young first appear on the undersides of the leaves. The adult lays eggs on the undersides of leaves where the hatched nymphs remain sucking the sap. These, somewhat resembling scale insects, are oval in shape, white at first, becoming yellow when grown at which time the skin splits and the adult, a tiny moth-like insect emerges. The adults fly about in great numbers when foliage is shaken.

Control: Malathion formulations or dust or sprays of DDT will abate this pest. It is well to spray in the nymph stage for an early control.

A Word to the Wise

No matter what spray or dust you are using, it is desirable to wear a simple face shield to protect your eyes and face. The kind used by painters when they are spray painting is very satisfactory. Most large paint stores and large mail order houses carry them. Any sulfur or alkaline material can cause your eyes to inflame, and all sprays—no matter what kind or who makes them—can cause physical damage if used unwisely or inhaled to excess. The proper kind of mask will cover the eyes as well as the nose; the thin skin around the eyes—in addition to the eyeballs themselves—must be protected from toxic materials.

Two more precautions: (1) Wear rubber gloves to protect the hands. (2) Read the label carefully before using any spray or dust, and follow its directions to the letter.

CHAPTER TWELVE

How to Propagate Roses

Most home gardeners find it simpler and less expensive to buy rose plants from their nurseryman or by mail than to propagate them. There are times, however, when growing your own plants may well be worth attempting.

You may want to produce a variety of rose that is not readily available on the market; you may wish to preserve interesting "sports" that have developed on one of your bushes; or you may wish to retire a favorite bush that is succumbing to old age or injury, by starting a new duplicate from its wood. Perhaps you simply wish to multiply the number of roses in your garden.

Besides these and many other practical reasons, the art of rose propagation can open up a very interesting hobby in the production, modification, and improvement of rose bushes. Many rosarians find the work fascinating.

There are three methods of propagation open to the amateur: by cuttings, by budding, and by planting seed. Of these three, growing from cuttings is the easiest method, but it is slow and unreliable. Budding is the surest and fastest and, at the same time, the most exacting method. Growing from seed is tricky, time-consuming, and thoroughly unpredictable.

One important restriction: It is against the patent laws to propagate any patented variety of rose by asexual reproduction without permission of the patent owner or his licensee. This applies to propagating for your own use as well as for selling.

PROPAGATION BY CUTTINGS

Propagation by cuttings is not difficult. However, if you plan to grow roses by this method, do it for fun and experience, rather than for results.

Self-rooted roses are rarely as vigorous as those budded onto established rootstocks, and, in many ways, are not too satisfactory. Furthermore, it takes two to three years at least to produce a good sized flowering plant by this process. Probably you will not root a large percentage of the cuttings you plant.

If you wish to try the experiment, here are the steps:

1. Make cuttings from wood of the current year's growth, in October or November when the wood is mature. In colder climates, make the cuttings in August or September.

2. The best cuttings will come from the middle section of a branch. Each one should include three nodes or leaf buds, which would make it 8 to 9 inches long. Prepare the cuttings by making an angle cut close above the upper bud and a straight cut about 1/2 inch below the lowest bud.

3. Remove leaves by trimming them off at a point about 1/2 inch from the stem. Do not pull them off. Remove bud nodes from part of cutting going in soil.

4. As you finish preparing the cuttings, wrap them in damp material until they are ready to be planted.

5. To prepare the growing medium, fill a deep flat or box (5 or 6 inches deep) with coarse river sand. Wet the sand thoroughly with water containing captan (1 tablespoon 50% captan to 1 gallon water) to prevent fungus growth. Press down the sand compactly with a block of wood.

6. Take the cuttings from the water, shake off excess moisture, and dip the basal ends in hormone powder to a depth of 1/2 inch. Tap off excess powder, but take care not to rub off the root-inducing powder.

7. To plant, make a slanting hole in the sand with your finger at a 45-degree angle. Insert the lower half of the stem carefully into the hole. Mound sand over the stem and press down lightly but firmly around the portion buried in sand. When planted on a slant, the cutting loses less moisture while rooting than if planted in a vertical position. Water the cutting again thoroughly.

8. Place the flat in a shady spot and cover with a piece of damp cheesecloth. As an alternative, some growers put

a large fruit jar over the planted cutting and remove the jar occasionally during the growing period for half-hour intervals. While it is rooting, keep the sand moist but not overly wet.

9. Pot up treated cuttings that have rooted (in 3 to 4 weeks) in a light soil. The potting mixture should be a sandy loam containing about one quarter screened leaf mold (preferred) or peat. No fertilizer or manure should be included.

10. Exercise great care in removing the rooted cuttings from the sand. The tiny roots are easily pulled or rubbed off. If necessary, loosen the sand with a gentle stream of water.

11. Keep the potted cuttings in a fairly warm, humid location for about two weeks. In that time the roots will have become established in the potting soil and the young plants can be relocated under conditions suitable for established rose plants, in the open ground if the weather is favorable.

Repotting into heavier soil and in larger pots can be done after about one month's growth in the light soil.

Fertilizing

Fertilizing can be started two weeks after cuttings have been removed from the starting flat and potted in the light soil. Use a half strength solution of one of the liquid plant foods and apply monthly until the plants have matured. The mature plants are easily transferred from the pots to a location in the rose beds.

PROPAGATION BY BUDDING

Probably the surest way for the amateur to propagate roses is to copy the method used by the commercial grower,

namely, to bud roses onto vigorous established rootstock plants. Many amateurs can equal the professional in the quality of the few plants they produce in this manner.

The process has two great advantages over growing from cuttings. Larger plants can be produced in two seasons, and the budded plants are likely to be more robust and flower more abundantly than self-rooted plants.

Budding is not a difficult process to understand. Essentially, it is a simple form of grafting in which a single bud, instead of a stem is inserted in a host plant. First, a cutting from an established variety of understock (see list below) is planted in the garden to serve as the rootstock for the new rose. After it has become firmly established, a leaf bud from the desired variety is inserted in its stem. In time, the new bud develops into a shoot; and when the shoot becomes established, the canes of the root plant are permanently cut off, and the new top takes over. From then on, the plant lives out its life as two plants in one—one variety in the ground providing the roots, a second above ground growing the foliage and blooms.

Budding is not a difficult art to master, but it does require timing, patience, careful workmanship, deft fingers, and a very sharp knife.

Selecting the Rootstock

First step in propagating by budding is to grow the root plant.

Commercial growers favor certain species and varieties that they have found capable of forming good root systems. In Northern California, preference is given to *Rosa multiflora* and Dr. Huey. In Southern California, Ragged Robin, *R. multiflora,* and Dr. Huey are favored. In other parts of the country, *R. multiflora* is the predominant understock.

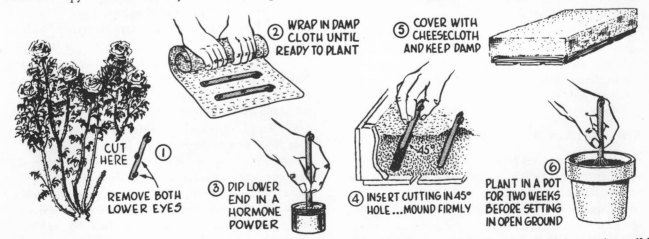

① CUT HERE / REMOVE BOTH LOWER EYES
② WRAP IN DAMP CLOTH UNTIL READY TO PLANT
③ DIP LOWER END IN A HORMONE POWDER
④ INSERT CUTTING IN 45° HOLE...MOUND FIRMLY
⑤ COVER WITH CHEESECLOTH AND KEEP DAMP
⑥ PLANT IN A POT FOR TWO WEEKS BEFORE SETTING IN OPEN GROUND

PROPAGATING FROM CUTTINGS: *This method is satisfactory for species roses and some climbers. Not good* *for hybrid teas or floribundas, which require wild rootstock for vigorous growth, satisfactory blooms*

Of these, *R. multiflora* is probably the easiest to obtain from the nursery, because some dealers sell this species for hedge planting. A single bush planted in your garden will supply you with an endless quantity of usable cuttings— but it may also take over your garden.

There is another way of securing a suitable understock that is probably easier than visiting your nursery. Simply wait for one of your roses to produce a sucker (which is, of course, a cane growing up from the wild rootstock); and instead of removing it as soon as it appears, let it grow to 4 or 5 feet, then remove it and use it for your rootstock cutting.

Planting Rootstocks

When you have secured suitable cuttings for your rootstocks, you should plant as follows:

1. Plant in December or January in mild-winter climates; in colder areas when frost is out of the ground.

2. Select pencil-sized, matured canes and cut into 8-inch lengths.

3. With a sharp knife, remove all bud eyes from the lower half of the cutting, leaving one or two good eyes on the upper half. Remove the leaves from the upper eyes by cutting the leaf stems ½ inch from the cane. *Do not pull off these leaves because this might injure the bud eye.*

4. Plant the cuttings in the garden where you want the specific rose to grow. This saves transplanting at a later date and gives the understock a good start.

5. Insert cuttings halfway into firm soil. Firm the earth around them and keep them irrigated. If it has established itself properly, the understock should be a substantial bush by June or July.

Preparing Bud Sticks

When your root plants are firmly established, you can move on to the second phase: budding-in the selected variety.

This can be done almost any time during the summer, but the controlling factor is the condition of the rootstock and of the plant from which you plan to take the bud. Both should be in active growth so the budding will "take." The understock should be plump and succulent so the bark will not stick to the woody core of the stem when it is peeled back. The bud should be taken from a shoot that has just finished blooming.

1. Select a shoot that has plump, mature but dormant buds. The best buds will be found in the center portion of the stem.

2. Cut off a portion of the branch that contains the buds and remove thorns and leaves. The thorns should separate easily, but if they do not slip off with finger pressure, cut them off instead of breaking them. Cut off the leaves about ½ inch from the stem.

3. Wrap the trimmed stem in a damp cloth. If it is necessary to store them for several days before you are ready to use them, place the wrapped bud sticks in the vegetable crisper of your refrigerator.

Setting the Bud

Now comes the delicate part of this procedure.

1. Thoroughly irrigate the understock a week ahead of budding.

2. Push the soil away from the rootstock to just above the level of the top root. Brush dirt off the stem with a whisk broom. The stem should be about ⅜ to ⅝ inch in diameter for ease in setting the bud. If it is thinner, you

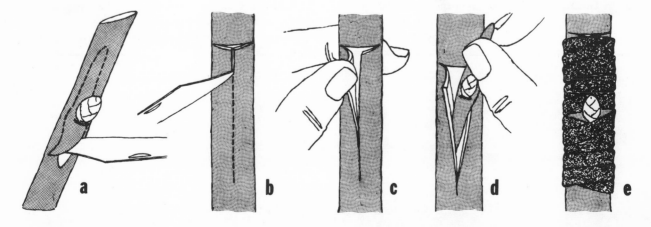

PROPAGATING BY BUDDING: *Method used for most commercial propagating. a. Cut bud from fresh cane.*

b. Make T-shaped incision in bark of understock.
c. Peel back bark. d. Insert bud. e. Wrap with raffia

will have difficulty fitting the bud into the slim stem; if it is thicker, you may find the bark too stiff to work easily.

3. With a sharp knife, make a vertical cut in the stem about 1 inch long and a cross cut to form a T in the bark. These cuts should be at a point midway between the roots and the lowest branch on the stem. Some experts recommend making the cut on the north side of the stem so it will be in shade during the heat of the day. Do not bud in excessively hot weather.

4. Peel back the bark to receive the bud.

5. Cut the bud from the bud stick with an upward slice of the knife. Cut upward from a point about $\frac{1}{2}$ inch below the bud to a point about 1 inch above, running the blade under the bud and cutting off a shield-shaped sliver of the stem. Some wood will adhere .to the bud shield, but it does not need to be removed.

6. Carefully slide the bud shield off the knife blade into the T cut, push it into place with your thumb, and fold the bark over the shield. If the upper end of the shield protrudes above the crosscut of the T, trim it off with the knife.

7. Tie the bud in place by wrapping the stem tightly with damp raffia. This wrapping should come close to the bud above and below but should not cover it. Wrap the raffia three or four turns both above and below the bud and fasten the loose end with a half-hitch. Professional bud setters use special rubber bands which can be procured from most large nurseries. Ask for "budding rubber." Rubber is by far the most satisfactory tie.

8. In three or four weeks, cut the binding and examine the bud. If it hasn't "taken" and is black and shriveled, set in another bud on the opposite side of the stem.

9. In January or early spring, depending on the local climate, cut the top off the understock. Using sharp pruning shears or a fine-toothed saw, top the stem about $1\frac{1}{2}$ inches above the bud union.

10. When the new shoot has grown out about 4 inches, pinch off its tip so it will branch out into a satisfactory bush. With favorable conditions, you should have blooms by late summer.

PROPAGATING STANDARD ROSES

Standard or tree roses are produced by what is known as "double working."

To form the upright single stem, a bud of *IXL* or *la Grifferaie* rose is set into the stem of a *R. multiflora* rootstock plant. When the bud has grown into a stem that is about 6 feet in height and has a diameter of $\frac{3}{8}$ inch, it in turn is budded with 2 or 4 buds taken from the desired rose variety that will form the head.

The buds for the head are set into the main stem at a height of 36 to 38 inches. These buds will grow out to form the typical flowering head. When shoots from these buds grow out to 4 or 5 inches, they are tip-pinched to encourage branching, and the central stalk is cut off 1 inch above the topmost inserted bud.

PROPAGATION FROM SEED

Growing roses from seed is quite difficult, and hardly worth the work. There is little chance of an amateur's producing new varieties of real merit from seed.

While the seeds of species roses will reproduce their kind, the offspring from hybrid tea seeds may have no visible resemblance to their parents. The breeding of roses from seed is an uncertain effort even for the expert.

To be successful in breeding new rose varieties in this manner, one must have a broad knowledge of rose heredity and genetics, extensive working experience, and the time and facilities to handle a great quantity of seedlings.

It is doubtful that even experienced plant breeders average more than one commercially successful new variety out of 5,000 seedlings they have grown to a flowering stage.

CHAPTER THIRTEEN

Societies and Exhibitions

It is characteristic of the rose grower that the better he understands the plant and the better the blooms he grows, the more devoted he becomes to the hobby of rose gardening.

A prime pleasure to which this hobby inevitably leads you is the camaraderie with others who have been caught by the spell of the queen of flowers. In company with other rose growers, you soon find yourself attending lively meetings of the local rose society, visiting the rose gardens of others, exhibiting your roses and comparing them against the prized blooms of fellow growers, or studying the art of flower arrangement. All of these and many other related pleasures lead to your deepening rose education and to your own increase in skill in producing roses.

But perhaps your greatest pleasure will come from the realization that you are reaching toward the goal of perfection in your own rose gardening efforts. In an age when the second-rate and the expedient are considered satisfactory aims by many people, it is stimulating to work toward the high goals that rose growing offers.

JOIN A ROSE SOCIETY

Membership in a society devoted to the study of the rose and its culture is the shortest route to success in rose growing. Association with members having long and varied experience should prove helpful to beginners as well as to the seasoned rosarian.

Most valuable of these affiliations is a membership in the American Rose Society and one of its many branches, if you are fortunate in having one in your community. This splendid national organization of 15,000 rose-loving members fosters the growing of better roses by amateurs.

For a modest annual fee, your membership entitles you to a monthly magazine, an annual, and various pamphlets and other services. The monthly, the *American Rose Magazine,* is packed with expert articles on rose culture and timely news of doings in the rose world.

The *American Rose Annual* is a cloth-bound, 275-page book that is filled with articles by rosarians which deal with new and old roses, their value, problems, and culture. It is illustrated with many full-color pictures of the newest and finest rose introductions. One of its most valuable features is a section entitled "Proof of the Pudding," which contains unbiased evaluations of practically all of the new roses introduced during a period of several years. This record is compiled from reports sent in by numerous amateur rose growers living in many parts of this country and in Canada. These reporters test the new varieties in their own home gardens and pass on their experiences and observations for the benefit of their fellow rosarians.

"Proof of the Pudding" is an invaluable buying guide to the new rose introductions, because it reports candidly on how the new roses may be expected to perform in your particular locality.

Application blanks for membership in the American Rose Society and information regarding its local branches can be secured by writing to the society's headquarters at 4048 Roselea Place, Columbus 14, Ohio.

EXHIBITING ROSES

A lingering visit to a rose show can be an inspiring experience, particularly for the beginning rose gardener. In the fragrant displays, you will see specimens of breathtaking beauty—most of them grown by spare-time gardeners like yourself.

Naturally, some gardeners can spare more time than others to the growing of roses; so each show has its acknowledged experts. They may be far ahead of you in their understanding of roses and in their skill in growing them, but you will find them approachable and more than pleased to answer your problem questions.

With ripened experience, you will probably want to enter some of your own best blooms in competition. You do not have to grow a great number of plants to compete successfully. In fact, the top awards quite frequently go to growers with small gardens, cramped in city lots. Indeed, the small grower often has an advantage over the large-scale hobbyist because he can tend to his plants with the intensified care and devotion that produces prize-winning blooms.

The production of rose blooms for exhibition should not be regarded as a separate art and practice. It should reflect the maturity of cultural skill you have acquired with the care of your own garden.

Grow all of your roses the best you know how and select your choicest blooms for the exhibition. There is no logical reason to cut back your plants severely just to secure a few big, blue-ribbon blooms. If you follow a sensible and regular program of feeding and watering, coupled with careful control of pests and diseases, you can grow prize-winning roses painlessly.

If you do enter roses in competition, do it in the spirit of good sportsmanship. Never question the decisions of the judges; accept them as final. Be considerate of fellow exhibitors and praise their winning entries. Enter exhibitions for the pleasure of the occasion—not as a ribbon collector.

Exhibitions for Beginners

To train beginners who are desirous of exhibiting their blooms, some rose societies annually hold simple club exhibitions for educational purposes.

The more experienced members judge and criticize the blooms entered by the beginners, who thereby learn how to pick, care for, and groom their flowers in order to present them at their best. The beginner also has a chance to compare his entries with those of other growers in a similar state of innocence.

If you belong to a rose society that has not put on such a show, urge the officers to plan one.

Qualifications of Exhibition Rose Blooms

Rose show judges consider five basic qualifications when judging exhibition blooms: form, substance, color, stem and foliage, and size. These points cover the basic qualification for bloom perfection of a rose for exhibition or for any other purpose. They can form your own standards as to what constitutes a good rose.

1. Form

This qualification refers to the shape of the bloom and the arrangement of the petals.

The bloom should have a full complement of petals for the particular variety. Petals should be gracefully shaped and symmetrically arranged about a well formed center. A high-pointed center is most desirable. With floribundas and other clustered types, the shape of the clusters and the arrangement of the florets should be attractive. The quality and number of the florets are also considered in making the award.

2. Substance

Substance refers to the thickness and firmness of the material making up the petals—the qualities that give them form, stability, and lasting stamina. A flower that is soft or wilts quickly, lacks substance. Good substance also implies a desirable texture, such as a velvety sheen on the petals.

3. Color

The color should be clear, clean, and attractive, and accurately characteristic of the variety. Weak, faded, blued, or dull tones are judged objectionable.

4. Stem and Foliage

The stem should be strong enough to support the bloom properly in an upright manner. Its length should be in relative proportion to the size of the bloom. A huge bloom such as CAPISTRANO, for instance, would call for a stem of about 12 to 14 inches in length to be in good balance, while a smaller bloom such as TAWNY GOLD would appear at its best on a stem of from 8 to 10 inches.

No properly conducted exhibition sets an arbitrary length requirement for stems. This is usually left to the good judgment of the exhibitor.

The foliage should be adequate in quantity and size for the stem and bloom, and its color should be clear and typical of the variety. The leaves on the stem should also come rather close to the bloom to avoid a "bare stick" appearance.

Insect or disease injury, tears or mutilation, unsightly spray or dust residue, are all preventable faults and judges will deduct points for them.

5. Size

Size shall mean that the bloom exhibited is a full-sized, representative specimen of the variety exhibited.

SCALE OF POINTS FOR JUDGING

Exhibition roses are rated by a point scale developed by the American Rose Society. This scale, which is used in the judging of practically all rose shows in this country, is as follows:

Form	25 points
Substance	20 points
Color	25 points
Stem and Foliage	20 points
Size	10 points
Total	100 points

Very few roses can be rated above 90 points in judging.

This judging scale of points is seldom applied to every rose judged, nor is this necessary. Its chief value is for use in close decisions, when judges do not agree, and for very important judgments such as "Best Bloom in the Show," and national cup or bowl awards.

GENERAL RULES

Well conducted rose shows issue a schedule giving the rules for the exhibition and a listing of the competitive classes in which you may enter blooms. These rules should be studied very closely and followed with care. Any deviation from the rules usually disqualifies the entry.

Here are the general rules followed in most shows:

1. Judges must disqualify exhibits which are improperly named, not named at all, or not worthy of exhibition.

2. Specimen blooms of teas, hybrid teas, and other exhibition types must have been properly disbudded. Side buds will disqualify the bloom. Evidence of very recent disbudding will be penalized at half the score of points for the stem.

3. Polyanthas, floribundas, grandifloras, climbers, species of old-fashioned roses may be shown without disbudding.

4. At the time of judging, an exhibition rose should be in the most perfect phase of its possible beauty. Usually this is when the bloom is half to three-quarters open. Tight buds are not judged as a bloom. A full-blown rose would carry a low rating.

5. Judges are presumed to be without prejudice or bias as to varieties, types, or colors, and should judge strictly on merits.

6. Grooming or dressing blooms is permitted if such treatment improves their quality and appearance, and is so skillfully done as not to be obvious. (Specks of dust, aphis or their eggs, should be removed from the petals with a camel's-hair brush. Often one or two superficial petals on the perimeter of the bloom are crumpled or off-color. These can be pulled off gently if the symmetry of the bloom is not destroyed. Remove all of the petal; do not leave a stub end. Grooming such as this should not be obvious.)

7. The use of oil or other foreign materials on the foliage is prohibited. (Lightly polishing the leaves with a soft cloth to remove spray or dust residue is not objectionable and may greatly improve the appearance of the specimen. Do your grooming before bringing your blooms to the show floor.)

8. Wilted or drooping flowers detract from the appearance of a show and should not be exhibited. (It is best to pick your blooms in the evening or early morning. After picking them, plunge them into a pail of warm water, about 100° F. Be careful that the leaves are not too crowded and that the flower is not under water.)

PHOTOGRAPHERS

Jerry A. Anson: page 41 (top right). William Aplin; page 41 (center left). Aplin-Dudley Studios: page 38 (bottom right). Ernest Braun: page 37 (top left), 39 (bottom). Carroll Calkins: pages 41 (top left), 44 (bottom left). Clyde Childress: pages 2, 9, 44 (bottom right). Robert Cox: page 61. Howard B. Hoffman: page 41 (bottom right). Theodore Osmundson: page 37 (bottom right). Maynard L. Parker: pages 38 (top), 42. Ron Partridge: page 3. John Robinson: pages 35, 39 (top), 40, 43. Blair Stapp: pages 8, 36 (bottom right), 41 (center right, bottom left). Mason Weymouth: page 36 (top). Herman Willis: page 75.

Index of Rose Varieties